by

HAZEL EVANS

Travel writer and francophile Hazel Evans has a long-standing interest in food and wine. She was once cookery editor for a national newspaper, owned a restaurant at Weybridge, Surrey and planted a vineyard at Arundel, Sussex. Now, with her daughter and son-in-law she runs workshops for writers and painters in Provence each summer where French regional food and wine is featured on the menu.

Produced by the Publishing Division of
The Automobile Association

Written by Hazel Evans
Consultant: Bridget Jones
Copy Editors: Barbara Croxford, Audrey Horne

Edited, designed and produced by AA Publishing.

Reprinted 1994

Distributed in the United Kingdom by AA Publishing, Norfolk House, Priestley Road, Basingstoke, Hampshire, RG24 9NY.

A CIP catalogue record for this book is available from the British Library.

ISBN 0 7495 0436 6

Published by AA Publishing, a trading name of Automobile Association Developments Limited, whose registered office is Norfolk House, Priestley Road, Basingstoke, Hampshire, RG24 9NY.
Registered number 1878835.

Typesetting: Microset Graphics Ltd, Basingstoke

Colour separation: Scantrans P.T.E., Singapore

Printed by: Printers Trento, S.R.L., Italy

Front cover picture: Foie gras

CONTENTS

This book employs a simple rating system for dishes and specialities in the A–Z sections on foods and drinks:

◆◆◆ something really special

◆◆ try it if you can

◆ worth a try if you come across it

ABOUT THIS BOOK

One of the pleasures of travelling is sampling the local food and drink. Whether your tastes are adventurous or conservative, this book will whet your appetite and give you a genuine taste of France. The perfect companion to any meal, it may change your ideas about what is on offer in this gourmet's paradise.

Not only will this book help you to appreciate the true flavours of the country, the practical information will enable you to cope with new or unfamiliar situations, taking the worry out of getting what you want.

France's regions are colourfully described, with the emphasis on local foods and specialities, and a look at the influences and traditions that you can still detect in them.

A comprehensive A–Z covers the foods you are likely to see in shops and markets and the dishes that appear on menus, with star ratings, to help you make choices. Where items in this list are mentioned elsewhere in the text, they are printed in small capitals, thus: CASSOULET.

There is information and advice on some of the best wines and the more unassuming ones worth sampling, along with an A–Z of other drinks, both alcoholic and non-alcoholic, also star rated.

The guide to shopping describes the different types of establishments and what services they offer, what you can buy and when it is in season. There are useful phrases and lists of groceries with simple phonetics to help you ask for them.

The recipes include some of the most famous regional dishes and will appeal to cooks of all abilities.

A short section highlights the types of food and dishes eaten on high days and holidays and advises on what is seasonally available.

Trying to understand the menu can sometimes be a nightmare. The section on eating out gives advice and phrases to use in a variety of establishments, as well as hints on how to order drinks. There are also tips on catering for babies and children, special diets and coping with a tight budget.

To round off there are more phrases, with a pronunciation guide, and conversion tables to help with shopping and cooking.

INTRODUCTION

No other country has influenced international cooking as much as France has. And it offers such a diversity of dishes that you need to return again and again to sample the specialities of each area.
Some of the dishes are influenced by countries beyond the French borders, from the hearty Teutonic-style dishes of Alsace to the Spanish influences that permeate the dishes from the Basque country, and the Italian-inspired ideas from Nice. But having been influenced by a neighbouring food, the French will add a touch that makes a dish entirely their own.
A concern with the variety and quality of French cuisine dates back to the arrival of Catherine de Médicis at court for her marriage to Henri II in the 16th century. The culinary arts were further advanced by her cousin, Marie, and like all courtly fashions, they spread from there to the ordinary French people.
Louis XIV took an interest too, developing the the custom of serving dishes in a particular order, and the French Revolution brought with it not only civil liberties, but also a higher standard of cooking for everyone.
French cuisine is noted for its sauces which enhance the texture and flavour of food, and herbs and spices are used on a large scale, as well as plenty of butter and cream. Wine is used in cooking all over the country, but as this is usually the local wine, it may make a dish subtly different from the same thing cooked elsewhere. Some of the best wines and liqueurs in the world come from France.

Eating out in France is an adventure. Even the simplest restaurant can offer a gourmet experience

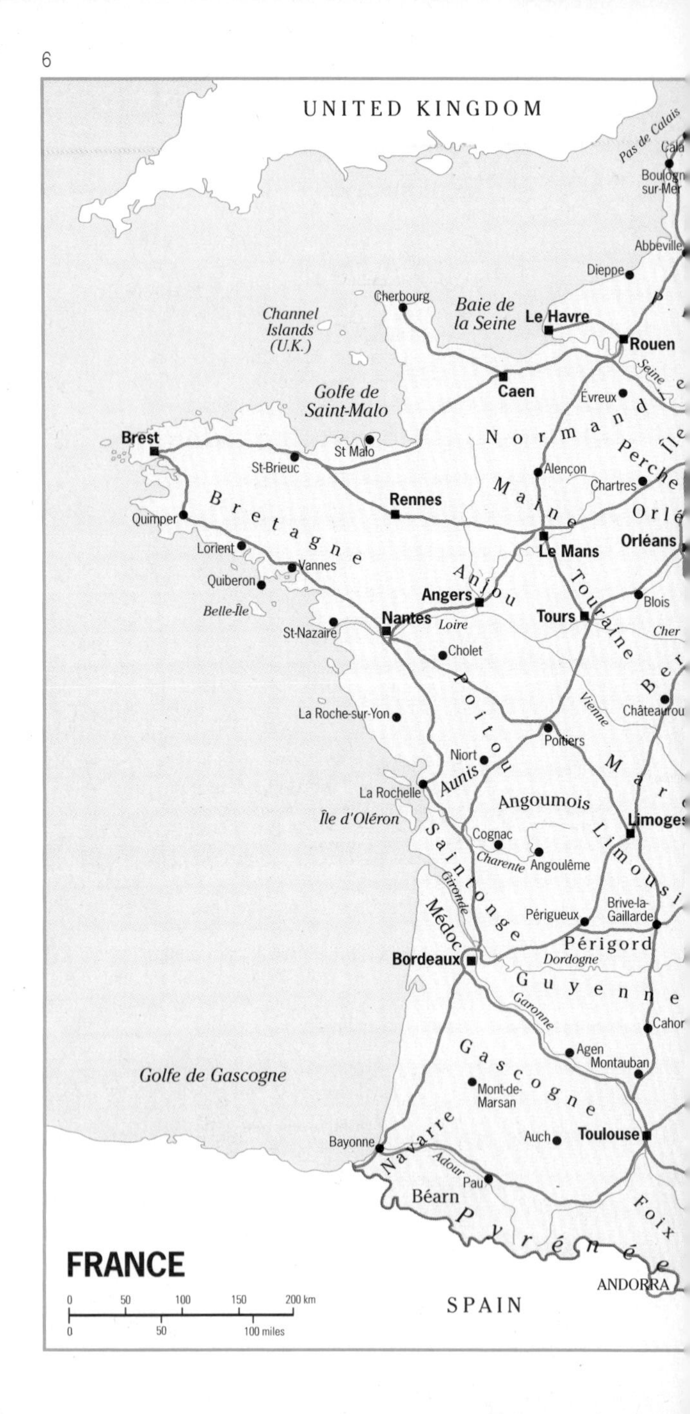
UNITED KINGDOM
Pas de Calais
Abbeville
Dieppe
Cherbourg
Baie de la Seine
Le Havre
Rouen
Channel Islands (U.K.)
Seine
Caen
Évreux
Golfe de Saint-Malo
Normandie
Brest
St Malo
St-Brieuc
Alençon
Perche
Chartres
Maine
Bretagne
Rennes
Quimper
Lorient
Vannes
Quiberon
Belle-Île
Le Mans
Orléans
Anjou
Angers
Touraine
Blois
Tours
Nantes
Loire
St-Nazaire
Cher
Cholet
Poitou
Vienne
La Roche-sur-Yon
Poitiers
Niort
Aunis
La Rochelle
Angoumois
Île d'Oléron
Limoges
Cognac
Charente
Angoulême
Saintonge
Gironde
Limousin
Médoc
Périgueux
Brive-la-Gaillarde
Périgord
Bordeaux
Dordogne
Guyenne
Garonne
Agen
Montauban
Gascogne
Golfe de Gascogne
Mont-de-Marsan
Bayonne
Auch
Toulouse
Navarre
Adour
Pau
Béarn
Foix
Pyrénées
ANDORRA
SPAIN
FRANCE
0 50 100 150 200 km
0 50 100 miles

BELGIUM
Dunkerque
Lille
Lens
Arras
Valenciennes
Maubeuge
Artois
Ardennes
LUXEMBOURG
GERMANY
St-Quentin
Meuse
Reims
Oise
Metz
Forbach
Lorraine
Châlons-sur-Marne
PARIS
Champagne
Nancy
Strasbourg
Melun
Marne
Moselle
Vosges
Alsace
Troyes
Chaumont
Épinal
Colmar
Mulhouse
Montbéliard
Auxerre
Dijon
Franche-Comté
Besançon
SWITZERLAND
Sancerre
Bourgogne
Bourges
Nivernais
Chalon-sur-Saône
Jura
Moulins
Bourbonnais
Loire
Mâcon
Bourg-en-Bresse
Roanne
Annecy
Savoie
Clermont-Ferrand
Lyonnais
Lyon
Chambéry
Puy de Sancy 1885m
St-Étienne
Grenoble
Dauphiné
ITALY
Massif Central
St-Flour
Le Puy
Valence
Aurillac
Cévennes
Languedoc
Rhône
Gap
Durance
Alpes Maritimes
Rodez
Avignon
Nîmes
Arles
Provence
MONACO
Nice
Montpellier
Carmargue
Aix-en-Provence
Cannes
Béziers
Marseille
Toulon
Côte d'Azur
Narbonne
Golfe du Lion
Perpignan
Roussillon
Bastia
Corte
Corse
Ajaccio
Porto Vecchio
Bonifacio

THE REGIONS OF FRANCE

French food varies greatly from region to region, and great store is set by the use of traditional cooking methods and fresh local produce. Such cuisine has its roots back in the days when France's provinces were independent of each other, with their own unique cultures and languages.

Normandy

Normandy (Normandie) has an abundance of good things to eat, guaranteed to scupper plans of the strictest dieter. Its long coastline, which yields a rich harvest of seafood, is lined inland by lush green meadows, grazed by dairy cattle, with cider-apple orchards and story-book timbered farmhouses.

Not surprisingly, Norman cuisine is inclined to be rich, being very much based on butter and cream. Mussels (*moules*) for instance, which are found in the bays of Mont Saint Michel and Isigny, are served in a cream sauce here, rather than with the usual light one based on wine. This is also one of the few areas of France where you are likely to be served salted butter, unlike the rest of the country where 'fresh' butter (unsalted) is manufactured.

If you are eating out, fresh oysters from Saint-Vaast-la-Hougue are a delicious starter. Staying with seafood, try the famous *sole normande* – a feast of seafood, including oysters and mussels served as a garnish for the sole which is coated in a cream sauce scented with truffles. If you are feeling more adventurous, sample other fish dishes like *marmite dieppoise*, a mix of fish and shellfish cooked Dieppe style, with leeks, cider and, of course, cream. Normandy also has its own version of SOUPE DE POISSON. *Limande* is lemon sole and is used for cheaper dishes, *lisettes* are small mackerel, landed at the port of Dieppe, and *demoiselles de Cherbourg* are baby lobsters.

Many cities in this region have their own special dishes. Look out for the famous roast duck from Rouen (*canard rouennais*), specially bred locally. Stuffed with a mixture which includes its own liver, the duck is served with a red wine sauce. You will find tripe, if you are fond of this particular dish, served *à la mode de Caen* with root vegetables, leeks, cider, calves' feet and CALVADOS. Tripe is also found in ANDOUILLETTES *grillées* from Caen.

Pork is often served Vallée d'Auge style, flamed in CALVADOS, then cooked with apples and cream. This method is used for veal and chicken; turbot, another delicacy, is often cooked the same way. Pork turns up again in a variety of pâtés, sausages and some famous smoked chitterlings (pork offal) from Vire. Another Norman speciality is BOUDIN (black pudding), especially *sanguette*, a more expensive version made from rabbit's blood, from the Orne.

Some of the great cheeses are from Normandy, notably the disc-shaped Camembert with its creamy taste and distinctive white rind. The rectangular Pont-l'Evêque, with its yellow–orange exterior, comes from Normandy too, where it is made near the picturesque fishing port of Honfleur. It smells more pungent than it tastes. If you do not already know it, try the equally strong smelling LIVAROT which is made in the cider country, the pays d'Auge. Livarot has a harder texture, a spicy flavour and a rust-coloured crust.

Mouth-watering cakes and pastries to try for dessert include *tarte normande* – a flan usually filled with apples, but you may find one made with pears, as a surprise. Then there are almond-flavoured custards to try too, often laced with CALVADOS. Almonds are used again to make MIRLITONS, small light tarts from Rouen, while whole apples or pears sometimes appear cooked in pastry, known as *chaussons* or *rabottes*.

Normandy lacks only one thing: vineyards – its climate is too cold and too wet. But it makes up for that with cider and CALVADOS. The cider is quite unlike some mass-produced ciders, being thirst quenching and full of character, but do not underestimate its potency. Buy *cidre bouché*, slightly sparkling cider made, like champagne, in bottles with wired corks. CALVADOS, the famous apple brandy, is often made in small copper stills on farms in the valley of the Auge. If you are touring, it pays to visit the farms in the Calvados area and buy direct. A tradition, when you eat out in Normandy, is to drink *'le trou normand'* between courses, a small glass of CALVADOS which

Normandy's most celebrated cheese

should be downed in one gulp. BÉNÉDICTINE, the famous liqueur, is made in Normandy by the monks of Fécamp Abbey. Liqueurs are also used in luscious chocolates made in and around Fécamp.

Ile-de-France and Champagne

With rivers abounding in fish and with one-third of all France's catch being landed at Boulogne-sur-Mer, it is not surprising that there is a huge selection of fish dishes to choose from here. First there is BOUILLABAISSE *du nord*, a type of fish stew, then there is MATELOTE, a freshwater-fish version to sample. Look out, too, for the delicious *cervelas de brochet*, sausages made from pike and potato. Eels (ANGUILLES) are served jellied in wine, laced with herbs and quite unlike London's Cockney speciality. There are freshly-caught trout (*truite*) to be had from the Vallée de la Course.

Turkey is often served in this part of France, now replacing wild duck from the River Somme, a traditional speciality which is becoming more scarce. Chicken is often served cooked in beer (*coq à la bière*) – evidence that Belgium is not far away – with juniper berries and, sometimes, a dash of gin added. Beer also appears in another favourite, CARBONNADE DE BOEUF, beef slow-cooked with onions and herbs. Pork appears on the menu a great deal and pigs' trotters from Sainte-Menehould are famous, served slow-cooked in white wine with herbs, then grilled. You may find sheep's trotters cooked this way, too. Continuing to be more adventurous, *petits gris* snails, small and dark brown in colour, are a local delicacy, and some of the best frogs' legs (CUISSES DE GRENOUILLES) in France come from the banks of the River Somme.

The soups cooked here are usually filling and the most famous one is *potage St Germain*, made from peas. *Potée champenoise*, another soup, does not, alas, contain champagne but only chicken, sausage and vegetables.

The charcuterie you will be served in restaurants, or that you may buy in the shops, tends to be on the hearty side. For instance ANDOUILLES and ANDOUILLETTES are much loved in this part of France, often eaten with cabbage and potatoes. And from the Ardennes comes a delicious ham, smoked to a deep rosy-red colour, which makes a perfect picnic food. You may find rabbit on the menu, too, and there is a special black sausage, *boudin de lapin*, made from it. Pâté on sale may well be labelled *potje*, a Flemish name.

This area of France is known as a pastry cook's paradise. It is from here that gâteaux like the famous SAINT-HONORÉ originated. Sweets – for example, *bêtises de Cambrai*, a type of humbug, and sugared almonds are also a speciality of the region.

You will also find some of the best bread in France here. If you like gingerbread, then you must try the local version, *pain d'épices*. Fans of spicy savouries should look out for *moutarde de Meaux*, a local granular mustard that goes well with cold roast white meat.

Although there are some delicious local cheeses to try (MAROILLES, for instance, with its orange crust), BRIE and the milder-flavoured COULOMMIERS are the two best known.

It is here that the greatest wine of all is made. Although some very good, strong beer is brewed in northern France, the world's most famous wine, champagne, is what you will most likely want to drink. When you have bought your glass of bubbly, you should accompany it with the elegant *biscuit de Reims*, a type of macaroon.

Alsace–Lorraine

This is pickled cabbage country: not only do the Alsatians eat *choucroute* (sauerkraut) but they produce it,

Tempting pâtisserie

and can it, in vast quantities. As you approach Krautergersheim, near Obernai, where the cabbage fields are, if the wind is in the right direction, you may notice that there is an unmistakable whiff of cabbage in the air. Alsace has what is called a continental climate with hot sunny days in summer but chilly nights. Hearty food, German style, is the order of the day with *choucroute garnie*, a dish of sauerkraut garnished with various types of sausages and pork, being the local dish. Just in case you feel there is not enough on the piled-high plate, they serve it with boiled potatoes too.

Other delicacies include *pâté de foie gras en croûte* (goose liver pâté wrapped in a pastry case) and goose liver pie seasoned with truffles. Goose is a staple on the menu, as are pheasants (*faisans*) and hares (*lièvres*). In addition, you will find essentially German sausages like CERVELAS made from smoked pork; *mettwurst* made from beef; and *knackwurst*, a frankfurter-style sausage. The most intriguing, however, is the *saucisse de Strasbourg*, the sausage from the culinary capital of the area. It is a smoked mix of both beef and pork, flavoured with caraway seeds. Also from Strasbourg comes *boeuf salé* otherwise known as *pikefleisch*, depending on how near you are to the border – smoked brisket of beef.

The Vosges mountains which divide Alsace from Lorraine act as a frontier of cuisine. Over on the Lorraine side the food becomes more French. This is the home, of course, of QUICHE LORRAINE, the famous egg and bacon tart, and the *tarte Lorraine*, which is more filling and spicy, made with pork or veal and onions. There is also a *tarte flambée*, which could almost be described as a bacon, egg and onion pizza. The dishes of Lorraine tend to be lighter than those of Alsace, containing eggs, cheese, and foods cooked in butter. Look out for *grillade à la Champagneules*, a kind of CROQUE-MONSIEUR, fried ham on toast, coated with a cheese and beer mix. And those with a sweet tooth should sample the jams, fruit tarts and pastries. Both Alsace and Lorraine specialise in fruits in syrup, based on plums, bilberries, cherries and raspberries, which are famous the world over. Plums of all varieties and redcurrants from Bar-le-Duc are also typical of the area. Cheeses are not a particular speciality here but you should try the best Munster, made on the slopes of the Vosges.

Local wines differ from those of the rest of France. Based on the Müller-Thurgau and Gewürztraminer grapes, they are slightly sweeter, more flowery and somewhat Germanic. Lorraine also has several spas and from here come mineral waters, VITTEL and CONTREXÉVILLE being the best known. A great deal of beer is drunk, of course, for hops are grown near by, and there is a huge selection of *alcools blancs*, clear spirits flavoured with fruits or berries. Quince (*coing*), sloe (*prunelle*) and raspberry (*framboise*) are definitely worth trying.

Made in Brittany: crêpe and cider

Brittany

The craggy coastline of Brittany (Bretagne) edges a land of contrasts where, not far from the wild and windy peninsula of Finisterre, is the garden of France. Its mild climate brought by the Gulf Stream enables the Bretons to grow early spring vegetables and, from late spring on, delicious strawberries from Plougastel. Melons, dessert grapes, wonderful walnuts and pears are all foods to enjoy in this part of France, which varies in climate from the rainy north, to the sunny beaches of places like La Baule.

Some of the best shellfish in the world comes from here; for instance, delicate Belon oysters from the Pont-Aven area, lobster (*homard*) and clams (*palourdes*). This is the home of HOMARD A L'ARMORICAINE, lobster cooked in oil with onions or shallots, tomatoes, white wine and brandy. Coquilles Saint-Jacques (scallops) also come from here, and the local equivalent of BOUILLABAISSE, the famous fish stew, is COTRIADE, white fish cooked with mussels, onions, potatoes, herbs and cream. If you have time, visit one of the picturesque fish markets such as those at Saint-Malo, Quiberon, or Loctudy, to watch the day's catch come in.

Breton chickens are good too, renowned for their succulence and plumpness, and pork is used for some stunning *pâtés de campagne*, RILLETTES and other items of charcuterie.

The Bretons seem to have a predilection for porridge, and you may find *bouillie* on the menu, a solid mix of buckwheat flour that can only be likened to the Italian polenta or, perhaps, Indian daal. Of course this is pancake country, and you can eat an entire, very cheap meal in a *crêperie* this way. Start with a seafood crêpe, move on to a savoury GALETTE, a heavier pancake made with buckwheat, then end up with one drenched in kirsch for a dessert.

Cheeses here are inclined to be mild, with PORT-SALUT and SAINT-PAULIN, with its bright orange rind, being best known.

Brittany boasts many traditional cakes, but the best known one is called *quatre-quarts* (four quarters), a light but firm sponge. It is often mixed with candied fruit, almonds and raisins.

No wine is actually made in Brittany, though its ciders, like those of Normandy, will make you think again about this refreshing drink. If, on the other hand, you want wine to go with your seafood, choose something from the Loire, just beyond Brittany's borders, a Muscadet, perhaps.

Finally, do not go home without a traditional plait of the famous red-skinned Breton onions which are grown near Roscoff.

The Loire Valley

The long, lazy Loire meanders its way to the sea through a mild countryside of castles, and caves – some of the best wine cellars in France – ending in the majestic port of Nantes. There are some 200,000 hectares/500,000 acres of vineyards here, producing wines as diverse as the fruity reds of Touraine, and Vouvray, a sparkling alternative to champagne. As you would expect from an area that produces great wines, the food from the Loire Valley is elegant.

As the area is laced with streams and tributaries, freshwater fish abound; pike (*brochet*), carp (*carpe*), salmon (*saumon*) and eel (*anguille*) are plentiful. Chicken, rabbit and pork appear, too, and the *Châteaubriand* steak is named after a small town here. You will find HARICOT DE MOUTON served too, which, strictly speaking, should not have haricot beans in it at all, for it comes from an old word *halicot* which means to chop. Look out, too, for appetising RILLETTES made from chopped pork meat, delicious spread on thick slices of country bread, as well as hare and partridge terrines.

This is a major mushroom-producing area, so it is not surprising that the CÈPES and CHANTERELLES appear in many local dishes, especially a salad of raw mushrooms. And if you

are there at the right time, eat locally grown asparagus, especially the Vineuil-Saint-Claude variety which grows in the fine sands bordering the river Loire, not far from the famous Château de Chambord.
Vegetables appear prominently on the menu and in the markets, pumpkins, potatoes and cabbage in particular. *Truffiat* is the name of a potato cake, and *bardatte* is a dish of cabbage stuffed with hare.
For dessert you will probably buy or be offered the speciality of the area, *gâteau de Pithiviers*, a puff-pastry tart filled with almond paste.
SAINT-PAULIN, the famous creamy cheese with a soft rind, is made in this area. Other local cheeses to look out for include the pyramid-shaped VALENÇAY, and Feuille de Dreux, a cows' milk cheese shaped like a Camembert and covered with chestnut leaves.
The wines of the Loire are legion; among the whites try Sauvignon, Sancerre and Vouvray. To go with shellfish, there is the famous Muscadet. But perhaps one of the best known drinks from this area is Cointreau, the orange-flavoured liqueur. See page 72 for more on the wines of the Loire Valley.

Burgundy
Beautiful Burgundy (Bourgogne), basking in the sun, is as well known for its food as its wines, which include Beaujolais, as well as the world-famous Côtes de Beaune.
Sample some of the good living here, for both game and fish abound in great quantity, and the white Charolais cattle, known throughout the world, produce superb meat. The ubiquitous pig, too, provides the usual selection of charcuterie and dishes to be found elsewhere in France. A speciality here is JAMBON PERSILLÉ – pressed ham layered with parsley and aspic – served cold. A strangely named sausage you will find around here, by the way, is *Jésus de Morteau* which tastes very akin to salami.
When it comes to dining out, start your meal with GARBURE, a hearty soup containing vegetables, bacon and sometimes sausages and beans, or a MATELOTE, freshwater fish made into a soup with red wine. Or, if you like snails, try them *à la bourguignonne*, served piping hot stuffed with garlic flavoured butter with parsley.
The dish that is probably most famous in this area is COQ AU VIN, chicken flamed in brandy then poached in good red wine with tiny whole onions and button mushrooms. Another delicious speciality is BOEUF A LA BOURGUIGNONNE, beef slow-cooked in a sauce made with young red wine. *Lapin à la moutarde* (rabbit in a mustard sauce) appears on the menu too, using the famous mustard from Dijon (remember to take a pot home) – see recipe page 108.
The rivers, lakes and streams of Burgundy are full of fish, so *quenelles de brochet* (patties made from pike), appear on the menu, as does *pochouse*, a stew made from a mix of fish in white wine – it becomes *meurette* when the wine used is a red one. Another classic Burgundian

savoury of a lighter kind is GOUGÈRE, a ring or small bun of choux pastry flavoured with GRUYÈRE cheese.
The most important cheese from Burgundy is probably the creamy, blue-veined BLEU DE BRESSE, though GRUYÈRE, unexpectedly, is also produced near by – often sold under the name of Comté – as well as in the Haute Savoie.
The orchards and fruit fields of Burgundy are the inspiration behind the wonderful fruit tarts you will find in the *pâtisseries*, including a tart made from bilberries (*myrtilles*). The fruit flavours are preserved too in EAU-DE-VIE, white brandy with plums, raspberries or bilberries. CRÈME DE CASSIS, the famous liqueur, is made from blackcurrants grown on the Burgundy hillsides. Mix it with white wine to make a drink called *Kir*. Candied fruits and jams are popular here too, particularly the delicious fruit-packed *confitures*, conserves made in Bar-le-Duc and Gevrey-Chambertin.
If the opportunity to sample home-baking arises, you may be offered *nonnettes de Dijon* (iced gingerbread cake) and the *madeleines* of Commercy (little sponge cakes).
Where do you begin with the wines of Burgundy? White wine names like Chablis and Pouilly Fuissé spring to mind, while for red wine drinkers there are the great red burgundies from the Côte d'Or and simpler reds from the Beaujolais district. See pages 71-2 for more on the wine of Burgundy.

Bordeaux and the Dordogne

This is the land of the goose, and good living. It shares with Normandy a tendency to use butter and cream in the cuisine, rather than oil. Also many dishes are cooked in goose fat.
This is a place to feast on truffles and FOIE GRAS, and these two ingredients are almost always included in any dish marked *périgourdine*. The truffles, considered a great delicacy, come from the nearby forests where they are sought out by specially trained dogs,

Dordogne geese, source of the notorious **foie gras**

and fetch amazing prices at the market. If you are there when they are in season, and decide to buy one, treat it like black gold, for that is what it is known as locally. To make your truffle go a long way – for it is unlikely you will want to afford more than one – place it in a bowl of eggs. Its delicate flavour will permeate their shells and, hey presto, you have a clutch of truffle-flavoured eggs for omelettes. In local restaurants you will probably find truffles featured in the famous local dish *brouillade périgourdine*, where they are cooked with scrambled eggs. You will also find plenty of CÈPES, large mushrooms, on sale in the markets.

Although the goose holds pride of place on the menu, it is mainly eaten in the form of PÂTÉ DE FOIE GRAS (goose liver pâté). The bird is seldom served roasted but is braised with wine and vegetables, served stuffed with plums (*oie farcie aux pruneaux*), or cooked and stored in its own fat in stoneware jars (CONFIT D'OIE). You will find ducks on sale, too, and turkeys which are becoming more and more in vogue in the Dordogne. Pork is also popular and you may also be served suckling pig. There are also splendid locally cured hams on sale from Poitou. From the bountiful countryside and forests around, come all sorts of delights like the guinea fowl (*pintadeau*), hare (*lièvre*), which is served jugged (*civet de lièvre*) and plenty of wood pigeons (*palombes*). Beef is good here too, and an *entrecôte à la bordelaise* comes with the classic sauce made of red wine, shallots and the essential touch of tarragon. The famous *pré-salé* lamb of Pauillac, from sheep grazed on the banks of the Gironde, is also delicious, served, almost inevitably, with truffles. This is also snail country; look out for them served Languedoc style, with nuts, anchovies and tomatoes. Good freshwater fish like shad (*alose*) and the barbel (BARBEAU) is available everywhere. A favourite dish in this part of the world is a FRITURE, a fry-up of freshwater fish. Another very filling dish from the Poitou is a *chaudrée*, a stew of conger eel and white fish cooked with potatoes, garlic and white wine. It was originally cooked in a cauldron (*chaudron*) – hence the name. There are oysters from La Rochelle and, as a curiosity, you could try lamprey (*lamproie*), the eel-like creature which comes from the estuary of the River Gironde. It has a poisonous thread that must be taken out before cooking, making it safer to eat it in a restaurant, where it is served with root vegetables and a wine sauce, rather than to try your hand at cooking it.

The lush green countryside yields plenty of succulent young spring vegetables. Later come green beans and those super-large Marmande tomatoes, a speciality of the area, that are so good stuffed. Above all, this is the place for delicious young broad beans (*fèves*). In late summer, shallots are plentiful too, and in the autumn the pumpkins (*potirons*) make their appearance. At the same time the fruits in season include greengages (*reines-Claude*) and yellow plums (*prunes*). Chestnuts and walnuts abound, and are used for both sweet and savoury dishes. This is one of the few places in Europe where you can buy chestnut flour (*pain de paysans*). Cows' milk cheeses come mainly from neighbouring Auvergne; locally made ones are usually goat (*chèvre*), the creamy Caillebotes and the CABÉCOUS, often served wrapped in chestnut leaves. Rocamadour, on the other hand, can also be made from ewes' milk, according to the season. On the dessert front, look out for pancakes made with maize flour called, variously, *tourteaux* and *cruchades*. Almond-based biscuits are a speciality of this area, so is FOUGASSE, a rich cake-type bread.

With the vineyards of Bordeaux on the doorstep, some of the best wines in France, the clarets – the Cabernet Sauvignons, Saint-Emilions and so on – are there for the buying. But try, too, the local wines of the Dordogne and its neighbouring regions, the deep dark red wine of Cahors, for instance. Cognac is the great brandy from Charente but if you are staying in the area there are innumerable local nut liqueurs to try, too. There is *eau de noix* and the sweeter *crème de noix*, made from walnuts, brandy and herbs. Other names to look for are *Brou de noix*, a spiced liqueur made from green walnuts, and *Ratafia*, made from various plants or fruit – drinks that you will find nowhere else.

Cleaning up the shallots

Auvergne

The lush green pastures and mild warm climate of Auvergne are ideal for cattle raising. Though winters can be cold, in the summer the cows roam on the mountain pastures watched over by herdsmen who live in *burons*, huts far from their home villages. This is where, in the past, they made the famous CANTAL cheeses.

Charcuterie is excellent here, for the pigs of Auvergne provide excellent sausages. Every town has its own local speciality, and it is worthwhile seeking it out: Saint-Flour, for instance, produces a delicacy called *friand sanflorain*, made of pork meat with herbs in a pastry case. There are pâtés too, made as smooth as silk or rough-cut, country style. There is black pudding with chestnuts (*boudin aux châtaignes*), peppered ham (*jambon au poivre*) and raw mountain hams (*jambons crus*). Food tends to be on the hearty side, starting with *soupe aux choux*, made from cabbage, usually with ham or pork. Dishes that are typical of this part of the world include *tripoux*, delicious mutton feet and veal tripe stuffed and seasoned with herbs and cloves; then there is *potée auvergnate*, a typical country stew containing a rich blend of vegetables, salt pork and sausages. Another great favourite is TRUFFADO, a cheese and potato pancake spiked with garlic, while *pommes de terre au lard* is a tasty mix of potato, bacon and onions with herbs. *Aligot* is another delicious potato dish made with puréed potatoes and CANTAL cheese. Auvergne is also proud of its country-made hams, and uses them in many dishes; lentils from Le Puy are often added to meals.

Jambons crus, ***raw smoked hams***

When the cherries are out in the spring you will find *milliards* and CLAFOUTIS, which is a baked batter pudding, on the menu and in the pâtisseries, featuring this fruit.

The cheeses are legendary and read like a wine list. Apart from the classic CANTAL, a semi-firm yellow cheese with a nutty flavour, SAINT-NECTAIRE, which comes in flat discs, has an elusive flavour of hazelnuts. Also nutty flavoured are such local goats' milk cheeses as GALETTE DE LA CHAISE-DIEU and *Brique du Forez*. The *bleus d'Auvergne*, the creamy blue sometimes green-veined cheeses, have a flavour that is fresh and slightly sharp, while the FOURME D'AMBERT is a veined cheese that was being made, it is claimed, even before Julius Caesar invaded Gaul. There are dozens of small cheese-makers still operating in the Auvergne, most of them on mountain farms, and it pays to keep a look-out for them when driving through the countryside.

It is well worth while trying the local wines here – the Côtes d'Auvergne produced near Clermont-Ferrand, the light reds of Chantuges, Corent and Châteaugay, for instance. If you want to try a bracing cordial, pick Verveine du Velay, which includes 32 plants, such as wild verbena, growing in the mountains. There are two types: the yellow which is sweet and subtle or the green which has a stronger flavour.

Provence

The very word Provence conjures up a picture of a sun-soaked countryside, filled with olive trees, sunflowers and herbs. And this, one of the largest regions of France, produces the most pungent flavours. Once you cross the line where the roofs of the houses change to those distinctive terracotta tiles, and the temperature soars, olive oil becomes the staple ingredient in which food is cooked. It is said that the Italians first taught the French to cook, and the nearer you get to the Italian border, the more often pasta appears on the menu.

The Mediterranean, too, exerts its influence, and Marseille is the home of some splendid fish soups, notably the traditional BOUILLABAISSE. This, it must be said, is more than just a soup. It is a whole meal, in which your plate is heaped high with a mix of seafish seasoned strongly with garlic and herbs, coloured by saffron, with a slice of bread on the top. Any number of fish may be used to make BOUILLABAISSE, but it must contain *rascasse* (scorpion fish) which looks like a miniature red mullet. Those who feel that the BOUILLABAISSE experience is too much for them should ask for SOUPE DE POISSON instead, when the fish is puréed, the taste less obviously fishy. To go with these soups and many other dishes, comes AÏOLI, a heavily garlic-flavoured mayonnaise. ROUILLÉ, is another name you will find accompanying some soups. This is an equally garlicky, but hotter, spicier sauce.

Basil is the south's favourite herb, and you will find it features in another Provençal favourite, SOUPE AU PISTOU, cooked with a mix of vegetables and a basil paste like the Italian *pesto*.

Aubergines, olives and anchovies are the staple ingredients of a number of Provençal dishes, the famous SALADE NIÇOISE for instance, when they are mixed with green peppers, tomatoes, sometimes tuna and hard-boiled eggs. The Italian influence makes itself felt with items like PISSALADIÈRE, a speciality of Nice, which is in fact a version of the pizza, usually made as a square rather than a round tart. Provence can be searingly hot in summer but in winter, away from the coast, the climate can be surprisingly chilly, and snow is not unknown.

Corsica

We have not included a separate section on Corsica (Corse) since the food is, in the main, similar to that of the South of France. It does tend, however, to be slightly spicier and more robust – as are the Corsican wines, particularly the rather heavy reds. Look out for wild boar pâtés, home cured hams – all kinds of charcuterie. The sheep's and goats' milk cheeses are good and, on the seafood front keep an eye out for items like sea urchins and squid.

A–Z GUIDE TO FRENCH FOOD

A

Abats
The generic French name for offal, liver, tripe, feet, heart and so on. The frugal French eschew waste and tend to eat parts of the animal others might throw away. So it is not surprising to find heads, lungs, stomach, feet, even testicles (ANIMELLES) served. The names for the ones you are most likely to come across, in case you wish to avoid them, are in this section.

Agneau
Lamb. *Agneau de lait* is milk-fed, that is baby lamb, while *agneau pascal* is spring lamb.

Agneau de pré-salé
This phrase is found in dishes all over France, but notably in Brittany, Normandy, Bordeaux and the Vendée. It is meat from lambs that have grazed on salty meadows washed by the sea. The meat is always served young and usually roasted, sometimes, but not always, without strong seasonings like garlic or onion. You may not notice any difference from other lamb in its taste, but it is sure to be tender and delicious.

Aiglefin, aigrefin
Haddock.

◆ Aigo
A Provençal garlic soup, similar to that found in Spain and Portugal. Traditionally served poured over slices of bread.

Aigo boulido
Garlic soup with an egg in it, and topped with croûtons or fried bread.

Aigo saou
Garlic soup with added fish and potatoes.

Aiguille
Also known as *orphie*. Needlefish or garfish. One of the many delicious Mediterranean fish that you find on French menus. Do not be put off by the colour of the bones – they are mauve when cooked (although green in the raw fish).

Ail
Garlic (plural *aulx*). Garlic is used liberally in French cooking. In the case of salads, you can always ask for it *'sans l'ail'*.

◆ Aillade
A sauce made from garlic and oil, found throughout the country in slightly varying forms. Often served with snails.

◆◆◆ Aïoli
The classic garlic mayonnaise from Provence (see recipe pages 95–6). You will find it served with *crudités* (raw vegetables) as a starter and also with a special dish that is something of an acquired taste, BRANDADE DE MORUE.

◆ Aioli garni
A special stew of salted cod (MORUE) from Provence. It also includes vegetables, maybe meat, and a garnish of snails.

Airelles
Cranberries, whortleberries or bilberries.

Allache
Large sardine.

Allumette
Match: but it is also used to describe very thin-cut potato chips. The same word is sometimes used for small sticks of puff pastry.

Evening dining in old Périgueux

Alose
Shad (fish).

Alouette
Lark. Under recent EC rules, the French are not now allowed to kill small birds like larks for food, but you will occasionally find canned lark pâté on sale.

◆◆ **Alouette sans tête**
Thin slices of veal or beef, rolled round a savoury filling.

Aloyau
Beef sirloin.

◆◆ **Alsacienne, à l'**
Food cooked Alsace style inevitably comes with *choucroute* (pickled cabbage), ham and frankfurter-style sausages.

◆ **Amuse-gueules**
Literally 'amuse-mouth': tiny appetisers, usually miniature savoury pastries – quiches, for instance – served with aperitifs in some of the more expensive restaurants. Most Michelin one-stars now serve them.

Ananas
Pineapple.

◆◆◆ **Anchoïade**
A pungent Provençal paste of garlic and anchovies (see recipe page 96). It is used as a spread on toast as an appetiser in southern meals or served sometimes with *crudités* as an *hors d'oeuvre*.

◆◆ **Andouilles**
Cooked pork sausage with strips of chitterling inside it. Served cold as a first course in restaurant meals. *Andouilles* are on sale everywhere. They can be rather chewy and not to everyone's liking.

◆◆ **Andouillettes**
Small chitterling sausages. Usually served hot with mustard.

Ange de mer or **angelot**
Angel fish. This is a member of the shark family but in culinary terms it resembles skate, since it has wing-shaped fins.

Anglaise, à l'
In the English way. Meaning boiled, or with boiled

vegetables, which shows what the French think of English cooking. The same phrase is, however, used to describe any dish that is typically British.

Anguille
Freshwater eel. *Anguille de mer* is conger eel.

Anguillettes
Very small eels served in the Basque country. The French are very fond of eels which they eat both hot and cold, and garnished with quite elaborate sauces.

Animelles
Testicles. Usually served fried, they taste better than they look, but are not everyone's ideal dish.

◆ Annot
A Provençal cheese made from ewes' or goats' milk.

Appellation d'origine
A form of quality control primarily reserved for wine but it can also be awarded to foods – Puy lentils or Bresse poultry and specific cheeses for instance. More information on the *appellation d'origine* system is given in the section on wines, page 68.

Fine specimen of globe artichoke

Arachide
Peanut.

Araignée de mer
Spider crab.

Arapède
Limpet.

◆◆ Ardennaise, à l'
Meat cooked Ardennes style, usually with juniper berries.

◆◆◆ Arlésienne, à l'
Fish or meat cooked Arles style with tomatoes, onions, olives.

◆◆◆ Armoricaine, à l'
Usually fish, especially lobster, cooked Breton style with brandy, white wine, herbs, tomatoes, onions.

◆ Armotte
Like Italian *polenta*, maize flour cooked in goose fat. From Gascony, it is eaten instead of bread or rice.

◆ Aromes de Lyon
A cheese with a strong taste, soaked in white wine, often wrapped in vine leaves.

Artichaut
Globe artichoke.

Asperge
Asparagus. *Pointe d'asperge* is asparagus tip. Asparagus is normally served with butter or hollandaise sauce.

Assiette
Dish, plate.

◆ Assiette anglaise
A mixture of cold meats.

Assiette de fruits de mer
A plate of seafood.

◆◆ Aunus
Small triangular cheese made from ewes' milk from Charente.

Aurin
Grey mullet (South of France).

◆◆◆ Auvergne, bleu d'
Salty blue cheese from Auvergne with a creamy texture. Made from cows' milk, it is sold in circular packs all over France.

Avocat
Avocado.

B

◆◆◆ Baba au rhum
A yeasted 'cake' soaked with rum-flavoured syrup. Found in most parts of France. If you buy one from a *pâtisserie*, be prepared to eat it with a spoon.

Badasco
Provençal name for *rascasse* (fish). Used in BOUILLABAISSE and fish soups but not usually served on its own.

Baguette
Long stick-shaped loaf of bread.

Baie de ronce
Blackberry.

◆◆ Baiser
Confection of meringues sandwiched together with cream.

Bajoue
Pig's cheek.

Ballotine
Meat pie or GALANTINE. Eaten cold.

Banane
Banana. Served sometimes with cream and kirsch (*bananes baronnet*) or with rum, sugar and macaroons (*bananes Beauharnis*).

◆◆◆ Banon
Small cream cheese from Provence made from ewes', goats' or cows' milk. Sold as flat discs or, more usually, in cylinders. The cheese is sprinkled with savory, wrapped in chestnut or vine leaves or placed on a strip of balsa wood.

Bar
Sea bass. There are more than 60 different names for sea bass in French, notably *badèche*, *cernier*, *bézuque* and *loup de mer*.

Barbadine
Passion fruit.

Barbe-à-papa
Candyfloss – literally 'father's beard'.

Barbeau
Barbel, an unexciting, bony freshwater fish which may be casseroled with wine, typically in the Loire and Burgundy areas.

Barberon
The name for salsify in the South of France. This long, thin root vegetable may be served with butter or coated in white sauce.

◆ Barberey
Soft cheese from the Champagne, cured in ashes.

Barbue
Brill, a flat fish, sometimes served baked in tomato sauce with vegetables (*brancas*); or fried in oil with tomato, aubergine and garlic sauce (*à la toulonnaise*).

Bardaloue
Fruit in vanilla syrup.

Barquette
Boat-shaped pastry, rather like a small tart or flan.

Basilic
Basil.

◆◆◆ Basquaise
Food cooked Basque style, with tomatoes, peppers, rice.

Batavia
A type of bitter lettuce (see also SCAROLE).

Making Beaufort cheeses

Baton
Small stick of bread.
Baudroie
Monkfish.
◆ **Bavarois**
A cream and custard dessert, usually with fruit.
◆◆◆ **Béarnaise**
Classic sauce made mayonnaise style, flavoured with tarragon. Originally from the Basque area, but now found everywhere. Often served with steak.
◆◆ **Beaufort, Beaufort de Montagne**
A hard Gruyère type cheese with few or, more usually, no holes in it. Made from cows' milk, from Haute Savoie.
◆ **Bécasse** or **bécasseau**
Woodcock. Served roast with truffles (*à la Diane*) or on fried bread with FOIE GRAS (*à la riche*).
Bécassine
Snipe.
Béchamel
White sauce, flavoured with bay or a hint of onion.
Bedeu
Provençal name for tripe.
Beignet
Fritter – sweet or savoury.
Belle-Hélène
Ice-cream and chocolate sauce as served with pear.
Belon
Breton oyster.
◆ **Belval**
A firm mild cheese with a shiny rind, from Picardy.
◆◆ **Berawecka, Bireweck**
Spicy bread roll from Alsace with dried fruit and kirsch.
◆ **Bergère, à la**
Chicken or meat cooked 'the shepherd's way' with ham, mushrooms, onions and matchstick potatoes.
◆◆ **Bethmale**
A hard spicy cylindrical cheese from Touraine, made from cows' milk.
Betterave
Beetroot. Sometimes served Provençal style with anchovies and hard-boiled eggs.
Beurre
Butter. Usually sold and served

unsalted in France, the exception being Normandy. *Beurre demi-sel* is slightly salted butter.

Beurre blanc
Sauce from the Loire made with butter, white wine and shallots.

Beurre de Provence
Not butter at all, but a local name for *aïoli*.

Beurre maître d'hôtel
Butter blended with lemon juice and parsley. Used to top a slice of fish or meat.

Beurre marchand de vin
Butter with red wine, meat juices and shallots.

Beurre meunière
Browned butter with lemon juice and parsley.

Beurre noir
Blackened butter. Often served with skate.

Bifteck
Steak. *Bien cuit* is well done, *à point* is medium done, while *bleu* or *saignant* is underdone, ie rare. *Bifteck haché* is French for hamburger, but nowadays you are likely to see it called simply a hamburger.

◆◆ Bifteck tartare
Chopped beef served raw with tartare sauce or raw egg and onion.

Bis
Brown, wholemeal, used in connection with flour or bread.

Biscotin
Sweet biscuit.

Biscotte
Rusk.

Biscuit
Sponge cake. A *biscuit à la cuiller* is a sponge finger, a *biscuit sec* is a plain biscuit.

◆◆ Bisque
Thick creamy soup, usually of shellfish, made with white wine, cream, tomatoes. If it is described as *bisque aux légumes*, it is a thick vegetable soup made with lentils.

Blanc
White.

Blanc d'oeuf
White of egg.

Blanchaille
Whitebait.

Blanquette
White meat cooked in a white sauce, eg *blanquette de veau*.

Blé
Corn, wheat.

Blé noir
Buckwheat. Used for some pancakes (*galettes*) in Brittany.

Blette
Swiss chard.

Boeuf
Beef.

◆◆◆ Boeuf à la bourguignonne
The classic dish of beef casseroled in red Burgundy wine with onions and mushrooms.

◆◆◆ Boeuf en daube
Beef braised with wine, onions, carrots, herbs.

◆◆ Boeuf estouffade
A type of DAUBE, or stew, cooked with pigs' trotters.

◆ Bombe glacée
Moulded ice-cream dessert, usually one flavour filled with another, for example *bombe cardinal* (vanilla and raspberry ice-cream).

◆ Bonbel
Brand name of a small mild hard cheese from Saint-Paulin, found on sale in most supermarkets.

Bonbon
A sweet.

Bonite
Bonito. A fish similar to tuna, but smaller.

◆ **Bonne femme**
Poached in white wine with mushrooms, eg *sole bonne femme*.

◆◆◆ **Bordelaise, à la**
Cooked Bordeaux style, usually in a red wine sauce with shallots, tarragon and bone marrow.

◆ **Bossons macérés**
A goats' milk cheese you may find locally in Languedoc, soaked in oil, white wine and MARC (brandy), with a rather strong, acquired taste.

Bouchée
A mouthful, for example *bouchée à la reine*, a small savoury vol-au-vent.

◆◆ **Boudin blanc**
A white pudding, a type of sausage. Served poached in a sauce or in wine.

◆ **Boudin noir**
Black pudding.

◆◆◆ **Bouillabaisse**
Hearty Mediterranean fish stew from Marseille. The liquid is often served as a soup, the fish as a main course. There are various versions of this, *bouillinade*, for instance, a fish stew from Roussillon with onions, garlic, peppers and potatoes.

Bouillon
Stock or broth.

Boulangère, à la
Oven baked, often in the case of meat, with potatoes cooked round it.

◆◆ **Boule de neige**
Sponge or ice-cream dessert covered with whipped cream.

Bouquet
A name for a prawn.

◆◆ **Bourdaine**
Apple dumpling with jam. Served as a sweet in Anjou.

◆ **Bourgeoise, à la**
Braised meat or chicken with bacon, carrots, onions.

◆◆◆ **Bourguignonne, à la**
Cooked Burgundy style. See BOEUF A LA BOURGUIGNONNE.

◆◆◆ **Bourride**
A white fish stew from the South of France. Served with AÏOLI or ROUILLE.

◆◆ **Boursin**
Commercially made herb, pepper or garlic flavoured soft cheese from Normandy. On sale everywhere.

◆◆ **Boursotto**
A pastry filled with vegetables, rice, anchovies and cheese, from Nice.

Bouteille
Bottle.

Branche, en
Whole, as in vegetables – broccoli, spinach.

◆ **Brandade de morue**
Paste from Provence made from salted cod, soaked until soft, cooked, pounded with olive oil and milk or cream. Garlic may be added. Served with fresh or toasted bread. The *brandade* may be browned in the oven before serving. Very much an acquired taste.

◆ **Brandade de thon**
Canned tuna mixed with haricot beans, from Brittany.

Brème
Bream.

Brème de mer
Sea bream.

◆◆◆ **Bresaola**
Sliced, dried, salted beef from the South of France.

◆◆ **Bressan**
A mild goats' milk farmhouse cheese from Bresse.

◆◆◆ **Bresse, bleu de**
Cows' milk blue cheese with

creamy consistency, made in and around the town of Bresse.

◆ Bretonne, à la
Cooked Breton style, in onion sauce with haricot beans.

Bretonneau
Turbot.

◆◆◆ Brie
Soft cheese with a creamy, sometimes runny centre from the Ile-de-France. *Brie de Coulommiers* is factory-made brie, while *brie de Meaux* is farm made.

◆◆ Brillat-Savarin
A mild classic French cheese from Normandy with a triple cream content and a buttery texture.

◆◆ Brioche
A sweet breakfast roll made from yeasted dough, with eggs and butter.

Broche, à la
Spit-roasted.

Brochet
Pike. Often served in the form of QUENELLES (fish dumplings).

Brochet de mer
Barracuda, a fine-flavoured white fish with very large, firm flakes. Good cold with mayonnaise as well as hot.

Brochette
Skewer.

◆◆ Broufado
A traditional beef stew with vinegar, anchovies and capers, from Provence.

Brouillé
Scrambled. *Oeufs brouillés* or *brouillade* is a dish of scrambled eggs.

Brûlé
Flamed.

Brut
Raw.

◆ Bugne
A sweet fritter from Lyonnais.

Take your pick for fish stew

C

◆ Cabassol/les
Lamb offal (head, trotters, tripe) cooked with vegetables and ham, a local dish from Languedoc.

◆◆ Cabécous
Round soft cheese from Périgord, made with goats' or ewes' milk.

Cabillaud or **cabliaud**
Fresh cod. See also MORUE.

Cabot
Chub (fish).

Cacao
Cocoa.

◆ Cachat
Round, rindless Provençal cheese made from ewes' milk, with a strong flavour, often aged in vinegar.

Cachir
Kosher.

◆◆ Caille or **cailleteau**
Quail. Cooked variously with truffles (*à la gourmande*), wrapped in vine leaves (*à la dauphinoise*) or with white grapes (*aux raisins*).

Cake
If you see this word on the menu, it means British style fruit cake.

Calamar or **calmar**
Squid.

Camard
Gurnard (fish).

◆◆ Camarguaise, à la
Cooked the Camargue way, with tomatoes, garlic, herbs, orange peel, olives and wine or brandy.

◆◆◆ Camembert
Famous round cheese with soft centre from Normandy but available everywhere.

Canard, caneton or **canardeau**
Duck. *Confit de canard* is potted duck.

◆◆ Canard, maigret/magret de
A fashionable dish, especially in the South of France, of thin slices of underdone duck breast. The breast should be taken from a duck which was fattened for its liver.

◆ Canard(s), salmi(s) de
Roasted duck, served in a white wine sauce.

Canard sauvage
Wild duck.

◆ Caneton rouennais
Roast pressed duckling.

Canneberge
Cranberry.

◆◆ Cantal or **Cantalet**
Salty firm cylindrical cheese from the Département of Cantal in Auvergne. Made from cows' milk, it is quite widely available.

◆ Caprice des Dieux
Brand name of creamy oval cheese from Champagne.

Carbonnade
Braised, sometimes fried or grilled, meat.

◆◆ Carbonnade de boeuf à la flamande
A famous dish of beef and onions cooked in beer, from the north of France.

Cardeau
Sardine.

Cari
Curry.

Carotte
Carrot.

Carottes vichy
Carrots glazed with sugar and butter.

Carpe or **carpeau**
Carp. Bony freshwater fish with a subtle, to some people unexciting, taste.

Carpion
A type of trout.

Carré d'agneau
Lamb chop.

◆◆ Carré de Bray
Soft, slightly salty, square cheese from Normandy.

Carrelet
Plaice.

Casse-croûte
Snack.

Casserole, en
Cooked in a saucepan, not in a casserole.

Casseron
Cuttlefish.

Cassis
Blackcurrant.

◆◆◆ Cassoulet
Pork, mutton, or lamb, sometimes goose, with bacon and sausage cooked with haricot beans in an earthenware dish, from Languedoc (see recipe page 104).

Freshly cooked from the barbecue

Cata
Dogfish.

Causalade, oeufs à la
Fried eggs and bacon.

Caviar blanc
Mullet roe.

◆◆◆ Caviar niçois
Anchovy, olive and herb paste pounded in olive oil.

Cédrat
Large citrus fruit with sour taste, from Provence.

Celan
Sardine.

Céleri rave
Celeriac. *Céleri rémoulade* is grated celeriac in mayonnaise.

◆ Cendré d'Aisy
Strong-smelling cheese from Burgundy, cured in ashes and MARC (brandy).

Cèpe
Wild mushroom. A large variety of fungi are eaten in France, many of them looking quite unlike mushrooms. You will find them on sale, fresh or dried, in greengrocers' shops and in the markets. They have a more pungent smell and taste stronger than ordinary mushrooms and are slightly chewy.

Cèpes à la mode bordelaise
Mushrooms cooked in oil with shallots, garlic and parsley.

Cerise
Cherry.

◆◆ Cerises jubilées
Cherries served hot, flamed with kirsch.

◆◆ Cervelas
Lightly smoked pork sausage with garlic.

◆ Cervelas de poisson
Fish loaf made with pike, from Champagne.

Cervelle
Brain.

◆◆ Chabichou
Sweet-tasting, very small goats' milk cheese from Poitou.

Champignon
Cultivated mushroom. *Champignons de Paris* are button mushrooms.

Chanterelle
Wild mushroom with a distinct yellow tinge.

Chantilly, crème
Sweet whipped cream.

Charbon de bois, au
Charcoal grilled.

◆◆ Chargouère
Plum pastry from the Bourbonnais.

◆ Charlotte
Hot pudding of apples baked with buttered bread.

◆ Charlotte Russe
Cold cream custard set in a mould lined with sponge fingers.

◆ Chasseur
Cooked in the hunter's way with wine, mushrooms and shallots.

Châtaigne
Chestnut.

Châteaubriand
Thick steak.

Chaud, chaude
Hot.

◆◆ Chaudeu
Orange flavoured tart from Nice.

Chaud-froid
Poultry, sometimes game, served cold in aspic or glazed with mayonnaise.

Chavanne
Chub. Freshwater fish, bony and slightly soft fleshed. Sometimes used in stews.

◆◆◆ Chavignol
Round goats' milk cheese from Sancerre, sometimes known as CROTTIN.

◆ Chester
Brand name of type of French cheese similar to English Cheshire.

Chevaine or **chevesne**
Chub (see CHAVANNE).

Cheveux d'ange
Vermicelli.

Chèvre or **chevreau**
Goat.

Chevrette
Shrimp.

Chevreuil
Venison.

◆ Chevru
Round cheese similar to Brie from the Ile-de-France.

Chicon
Chicory.

Chicorée or **frisée**
Curly endive.

◆◆ Chocart or **choquart**
Apple pastry flavoured with spice and lemon, from Brittany.

Chocolat
Chocolate. *Un chocolat* is a cup of hot chocolate.

Goats' milk cheeses. Look out for local ones in the regions

◆◆◆ **Chorizo**
Spanish style highly seasoned sausage found in the South of France. Used sometimes in COUSCOUS (see recipe pages 105–6).
◆◆ **Choron, sauce**
Béarnaise sauce coloured with tomato purée.
◆ **Chotenn bigoudenn**
Roast pig's head with garlic.
Chou
Cabbage.
Choucroute
Sauerkraut.
Chou-fleur
Cauliflower.
Choumarin/chou de mer
Seakale.
Chou-navet
Swede.
Chou-rave
Kohlrabi.
Choux brocolis
Broccoli.
Choux de Bruxelles
Brussels sprouts
Ciboule
Spring onion.
Ciboulettes or **cives**
Chives.
Citron
Lemon (*limon* is a lime, not a lemon).
Citrouille
Pumpkin.
Civet
A thick stew, thickened by using the blood of the animal.
◆◆ **Civet de lièvre**
Jugged hare.
◆◆◆ **Clafoutis**
Classic baked batter pudding with cherries which comes originally from Limousin (see recipe pages 109–10).
Clamart
Served with artichoke hearts filled with peas.
◆ **Claquebitou**
Herb flavoured goats' milk cheese from Burgundy.
Clavelado
Another name for RAIE (ray or skate).
Cochon de lait
Suckling pig.
Coco
Coconut.
Cocotte, en
Slow-cooked in a sealed pot or heavy, lidded saucepan.
Coeur
Heart.
Coeur à la crème
Cream cheese served with sugar.
Coeur de filet
Prime cut of beef.
Coing
Quince.
Colimaçon
Snail.
Colin
Hake.
Colineau
Codling.
◆ **Colombière**
Mild smooth dish-shaped cheese made with cows' milk, from Savoie.
Compote
Stewed fruit.
Concombre
Cucumber.
Confit
Preserve, usually of fruit, in sugar.
◆◆ **Confit d'oie**
Goose, duck or pork preserved in its own fat.
Congre
Conger eel.
Consommé
Clear soup.
◆ **Consommé julienne**
Clear soup with thin strips of onion, turnip, celery, etc.

◆◆ Consommé madrilène
A clear meat soup flavoured with tomato juice.

Contre-filet
Beef sirloin fillet.

Coq
Cockerel.

◆◆◆ Coq au vin
Chicken cooked in red wine with glazed shallots or small onions and button mushrooms.

◆◆ Coq au vin jaune
A chicken dish from Arbois, cooked in local white wine with cream and fungi.

Coq de bruyère
Grouse.

Coque, à la
Cooked in the shell, eg *oeuf à la coq* (boiled egg).

Coquillages
Shellfish.

◆◆ Coquille Saint-Jacques
Scallop. Often cooked with cheese sauce or a white wine and cream sauce and served in its shell (see recipe page 103).

Corbeille de fruits
Fruit basket.

Corne
A type of brioche from the Nantes area.

Corne grecque
Okra or lady's fingers.

Cornichon
Gherkin.

Côte
Rib, chop.

Côtelette
Chop or cutlet, usually lamb.

Cotignac
Quince jelly. Eaten as a sweet, in squares.

◆◆◆ Cotriade
Breton stew from a mixture of fish with onions, potatoes, cream.

Cou
Neck.

◆ Coudenat
Pork sausage from southwest France. Eaten hot, in slices.

◆◆ Couhé-Vérac
Goats' milk cheese from Poitou, served wrapped in chestnut leaves.

Coulis
Thick purée, often tomato, also made from fruit. Served as a sauce.

◆◆◆ Coulommiers
Creamy centred, disc shaped cheese from Coulommiers in the Ile-de-France.

◆ Coupe Jacques
Strawberry and lemon ice-cream topped with fruit in kirsch.

Courge
Squash, gourd.

Courge à la moelle
Vegetable marrow.

Couronne de côtelettes rôties
Roast crown of lamb.

Court-bouillon
Stock of herbs, vegetables and white wine used for poaching fish or in fish dishes.

◆◆◆ Couscous
Cooked, rolled grains of semolina, steamed over a stew of vegetables, chicken and lamb served with HARISSA sauce – a hot, spicy condiment. A dish originally from North Africa served in many cafés and brasseries throughout France (see recipe pages 105-6).

Coussinet
Cranberry.

Crabe
Crab.

◆ Crabe froide à l'anglaise
Dressed crab.

Crécy, à la
Soup featuring carrots.

Crème
Cream.

Crème: Cream and Creamy Concoctions

Although *crème* means cream and dishes *à la crème* have cream in them, the term is also used for custard mixtures which are not necessarily made with cream. Here is a run through the main examples.

Crème, à la With cream, in a cream sauce.
Crème anglaise Egg custard.
Crème au beurre French butter cream, enriched with egg yolks and very sweet.
Crème brûlée Creamy egg custard with crisp topping of burnt sugar.
Crème caramel Set egg custard, turned out with caramel topping.
Crème Chantilly Sweetened whipped cream.
Crème fouettée Whipped cream.

A rich display

Crème fraîche Fresh, slightly soured cream.
Crème à la vanille Egg custard flavoured with vanilla.
Crème pâtissière Confectioner's custard. A thick custard enriched with cream, used for filling tarts and pastries, also gâteaux.

Crêpe
Thin pancake, sweet or savoury.
Crêpe dentelle
Very thin pancake from Brittany.
◆◆ **Crêpe Suzette**
Dessert pancake flamed in Cointreau with orange sauce.
◆ **Crépinette**
Small flat sausage from the Bordeaux area. Often served with oysters.
Cresson
Watercress.
Crevette
Shrimp, prawn.
Crevette grise
Shrimp.
Crevette rose
Prawn.
Crevette rouge
Large red prawn.
Croissant
Flaky breakfast crescent made in the same way as puff pastry, only with yeast dough and butter. The layers resemble puff pastry but the dough should be more substantial – slightly bread-like. Generally eaten with CONFIT.
Croquant
Crunchy. Also name for types of PETIT FOUR and honey biscuits.
Croque au sel
Eaten raw, with salt.
◆ **Croque-madame**
Toasted ham and cheese sandwich with fried egg.

◆ Croque-monsieur
Toasted cheese and ham sandwich.

◆ Croquette
Fried meat cake or fish cake, coated in breadcrumbs.

◆◆ Crottin
Small ball-shaped goats' milk cheese from the Loire. A name that appears increasingly on the menu. Often served grilled as a starter, sometimes arranged on a bed of green salad.

Croupion
'Parson's nose' of chicken or other poultry.

Croustade
Casing of fried bread, or pastry.

Croustille
Snack of fried potato slices.

Croûte
Crust of bread as a base, or pastry base.

Croûtons
Tiny squares of fried or toasted bread. Used as garnish for soup and added to warm salads.

◆ Cruchades
Sweet corn-meal fritters from southwest France.

◆◆ Crudités, assiette de
Raw young vegetables usually served with a delicious dip of garlic flavoured mayonnaise. Vegetables include strips of carrot, turnip, pepper, cucumber and celery with cauliflower florets, radishes, spring onions, broad beans and tomatoes.

Crustacé
Shellfish, for example lobster, crayfish, prawn.

Cuisse
Thigh.

Cuisse de poulet
Drumstick of chicken.

Cuisseau
Leg of veal.

◆◆ Cuisses de grenouilles
Frogs' legs. Tasting very much like chicken, they are usually sautéed with garlic or served with cream sauce.

Cuit
Cooked; for example, steak *bien cuit* (well done).

Cul
Chump chop.

Culotte
Rump steak of beef.

D

Dariole
Form of cream pastry, or custard cooked in a small bucket-shaped mould.

Darne
Thick fish steak.

Datte
Date.

◆◆◆ Daube
Meat, usually beef, braised slowly in red wine, herbs, carrots and onions. A Provençal *daube* often has orange peel included. By tradition it is cooked overnight in a closed pot over a slow fire.

◆◆ Dauphinoise, à la, dauphine
Usually potatoes sliced and baked in milk. It makes a very filling accompaniment to any meal or, sprinkled with cheese, can be served as a lunch dish.

Daurade
Sea bream.

Demi-sel
Slightly salt cream cheese.

◆ Diable
Usually kidneys or *poussins*, split, flattened, then grilled and served with hot pepper and vinegar sauce.

Room for everything in the barn

◆◆ Dieppoise, à la
Fish, often sole, cooked the Dieppe way in white wine sauce, garnished with shellfish. Some of the best seafood in the world is from the Dieppe area.

◆◆ Dijonnais
Meat or poultry, often rabbit or chicken, cooked with mustard sauce. It is important that the mustard used is the Dijon variety, not the fiercer varieties.

Dinde or **dindon**
Turkey. Not eaten as much in France as it is in Britain and the US, but found in country areas like the Dordogne.

Dorade
Sea bream.

Dorée
John Dory (fish).

Dur
Hard, that is *oeuf dur* (hard-boiled egg).

◆ Duxelles
A savoury mix of mushrooms and shallots cooked in butter until they virtually become a paste. Used as a base for some sauces and casseroles.

E

◆ Ecarlate
Salted, pickled meat, usually tongue. Found sometimes on sale in *traiteurs* or *charcuteries* (see page 88).

Echalote
Shallot. A mild more elegant form of onion, used extensively in French cookery. It gives a more subtle taste to casseroles, sauces and other dishes than the onion does.

Echine
Chine, loin of pork.

◆ Echourgnac
Small yellow-rinded cheese with holes in it, from Périgord.

Ecrevisse
Freshwater crayfish with a delicious slightly sweet taste. France's many freshwater rivers, streams and lakes yield a rich harvest of crayfish, however the virus sweeping

through Europe may affect availability.

Eglefin
Haddock.

◆ Emincé
Thinly sliced. Slivers of meat or poultry reheated in sauce. Many people mis-read this word on the menu and reject it, thinking they are going to be presented with mince.

◆ Emmenthal
Large wheel-shaped cheese with a honeycomb texture and slightly sweet taste that is similar to, and usually cheaper than, GRUYÈRE. You can use it with great success in a fondue, for instance.

◆◆◆ Enchaud
Baked garlic-flavoured pork and pigs' trotters with truffles from Périgord, a real country dish.

Encornet
Squid.

Encre
Black ink of octopus or squid. Often used in Mediterranean seafood dishes.

Snails, archetypal French fare

Endive
Chicory, the slightly bitter vegetable with long leaves of pale yellow packed close together. Used raw in salads or braised (*endives à l'étuvée*). *Endives au jambon* are braised heads of chicory wrapped in ham.

Entremets
Sweets.

Epaule
Shoulder, usually of lamb (*épaule d'agneau*).

Epice
Spice.

Epinard
Spinach.

◆◆ Epoisses
Flat cylindrical cheese from Burgundy. Made from cows' milk, it has an orange-red rind and is sometimes served cured in EAU-DE-VIE.

Escalope
Flattened slice of veal or poultry breast, often served fried.

◆ Escalope à la viennoise
Veal dipped in egg and breadcrumbs, then sautéed. Although this is not a French but an Italian dish, it appears very often on the cheaper tourist menus.

◆◆◆ Escalope normande Vallée d'Auge
Veal or chicken breast served with cream, CALVADOS and apple. A delicious but very rich dish from Normandy.

Escargot
Snail. The best snails are said to come from Burgundy, but now they are imported from various countries including Turkey and even England. Snails have very little flavour and a slightly rubbery texture – rather like whelks or winkles.

◆◆ Escargots à la bourguignonne
Snails stuffed with garlic butter and parsley.

Escarole
An extra curly leaved form of endive.

◆◆ Espadon
Swordfish. This has a rather dry, meat-like texture but is very good grilled, served with melted butter.

◆ Espagnole, sauce
A brown sauce made with bacon, carrots, onions, wine, herbs and spices. Served with meat or pasta.

Esprot
Sprat.

Esquinade
Spider crab.

◆◆ Estouffade
Basically a pot-roasted steak. Meat, usually beef, often cooked in one steak rather than cut into pieces, braised slowly and for a long time in a closed pot until very tender.

Estragon
Tarragon.

Exocet (poisson volant)
Flying fish, with fins that resemble wings and the ability to skim above water. The flesh is flavoursome and often treated as mackerel.

F

◆◆ Faisan, faisandeau or **faisane**
Pheasant. It is served fairly extensively in France. Roast pheasant (*faisan rôti*), stewed pheasant (*faisan en cocotte*) and other local styles of cooking are used.

◆◆◆ Far
Rum flavoured flan or tart with an ancient name which comes from Brittany.

Farce, farci
Stuffing, stuffed.

◆◆ Farci niçois
A chic form of RATATOUILLE. Stuffed courgettes, aubergines, tomatoes and onions, cooked slowly in olive oil.

Faséole
Kidney bean.

Faux-filet
Piece of beef sirloin

Faverolles
A name given to haricot beans in the South of France. They are used in local dishes such as CASSOULET.

◆◆ Fechun
Pork-stuffed cabbage, a hearty dish from the Franche-Comté area, near the German border.

Fenouil
Fennel. A vegetable that is used extensively in France. It has a distinctive aniseed taste.

◆ Ferchuse
Pork offal cooked in red wine with potatoes and onions, from Burgundy. Traditionally the heart and lungs from the main part of the meal.

◆ Fermière, à la
Meat, sometimes chicken, braised with mixed vegetables.

◆◆◆ Figue
Fig. Raw green figs make a delicious dessert, served in summer in the south. Sometimes eaten as a starter with ham.

Filet mignon
Small fillet steak.

Fines herbes
Finely chopped herbs. Used for flavouring, particularly omelettes. Usually parsley, chervil, tarragon and chives.

Take home some foie gras

Flageolet
Small French bean. Oval in shape and pale green they are often served with lamb.

◆◆ Flamande
In the Flemish way. A hearty meal of meat with braised root vegetables, cabbage and bacon.

Flambé
Flamed in brandy or some other spirit; often done to steak or pancakes. This practice is usually only carried out in the more expensive restaurants and does little to improve the flavour of food.

◆ Flan
A sweet or savoury flan of the quiche variety. The name is also often used, particularly in the south, for a rather heavy type of egg custard, a less delicate version of crème caramel.

Flétan
Halibut.

Flondre
Flounder.

Florentine
Food, often gently poached eggs, cooked with spinach, sometimes with cheese sauce. It is also the name for small chocolate coated biscuits.

Foie
Liver.

◆◆ Foie gras
Goose liver. *Pâté de foie gras* (goose liver pâté) sometimes has truffles added, a speciality of the Landes district. The geese are force-fed with grain so that their livers become enlarged to produce the *foie* in large quantities. Graphic pictures of the process, on hoardings by the roadside, tend to put visitors off the product rather than encouraging them to buy it.

Fond
Base, eg *fond d'artichaut*, the part that is eaten last, once the leaves have been drained of their goodness. Sometimes *fond d'artichaut* is served CLAMART, with a little heap of peas in the middle, as a garnish for a dish.

◆ Fondu au marc
Sometimes called *fondu aux raisins*, a type of processed cheese from Savoie. Sold in discs, it is covered with a distinctive rind of grape pips.

◆◆ Fondue
A hot sauce of Gruyère cheese, white wine and kirsch, from Savoie. Cakes of bread are used for dipping.

◆◆ Fondue bourguignonne
Pieces of steak cooked on forks in boiling oil with a variety of flavoured sauces to accompany them. The meat must be of top quality to stand this treatment,

and is best marinated beforehand. The sauces range from curry-flavoured mayonnaise to tomato sauce. The dish came originally from Burgundy, and is frequently found served at ski resorts.

◆ Foudjou

Strong goats' milk cheese with brandy and garlic, served with potatoes. This is an extremely pungent meal from Languedoc.

Fougasse

A type of bread, sometimes pastry (varies according to region). The *fougasse* of Provence resembles a lung, with its network of large holes.

Four, au

Baked in the oven, sometimes roasted.

◆◆ Fourme

Name given to a number of cheeses from Auvergne made from cows' milk. *Fourme d'Ambert* is a cylindrical blue-veined cheese. *Fourme de Montbrison*, sometimes called *fourme de Cantal*, has a sharper taste.

Frais

Fresh, cool.

Fraise

Strawberry.

◆◆◆ Fraises des bois

Wild strawberries. They are tiny and have a delicious, perfumed, sweet flavour. Often served as a dessert.

◆◆ Fraises Romanoff

A dish of fresh strawberries soaked in liqueur and orange juice, with whipped cream on top. Very easy to prepare.

Framboise

Raspberry.

Frangipane

Almond-flavoured confectioner's custard. Used in cakes and gâteaux and, occasionally, as a lining to a *tarte*, a buffer between the pastry and the topping. It looks rather like egg custard and tastes strongly of vanilla.

Frappé

Iced, served on crushed ice.

◆ Frappo

Casseroled ox tripe from Languedoc. Not a dish to tackle unless you are extremely hungry.

◆ Fréchure

Casserole of pigs' lungs, from Vivarais.

Fressure

Pig or calf offal, used extensively in French country cooking.

Friandise

Petit four, sweet.

◆ Fricassée

Chopped white meat, ie veal or chicken, cooked in thick white sauce.

◆ Fricaude

Stew of pigs' offal from Lyonnais.

Frisée

Curly, such as the leaves of endive, parsley.

Frit

Fried.

Frites

Chips. Frequently sold on camp sites and at roadside stalls.

Friture

A pile of fried food, usually small fish.

Froid

Cold.

Fromage

Cheese. France has a different brand of cheese for each day of the year, and the best ones are those given an AOC (*Appellation d'Origine Contrôlée*) just like wines.

See **The Regions of France** (pages 8–19) for descriptions of many local cheeses. Also see under individual cheeses in this A–Z listing.

◆ Fromage à la croûte
The French equivalent of Welsh rarebit (toasted cheese) using slices of rather soft bread.

Fromage de porc
See PORC.

◆◆ Fromage d'Italie
Not a cheese but something very different – a dish made with pig's liver.

◆ Fromage du curé
Cows' milk cheese from the Nantes area of Brittany. It is square and has a strong smell.

Fromaget
Cheesecake.

◆◆◆ Fruit de mer
Shellfish. The plural, *fruits de mer*, usually means a plate piled high with a selection of shellfish including, if you are lucky, some oysters, prawns and even lobster. It comes accompanied by instruments for extracting meat out of lobsters' claws, for cracking shells and so on.

Fruits rafraîchis
Fruit salad.

Fumé
Smoked.

Fumet
Strong fish stock.

G

◆ Galantine
Meat or poultry, usually stuffed, poached and pressed in aspic. Eaten as a first course or as part of an *hors d'oeuvre*. It is also the name of a type of cheese from northern France.

◆◆◆ Galette
A pancake made with buckwheat flour, a Breton speciality. The batter is spread on a hot griddle, using a special wooden scraper, until it is thin and even. The flipped cooked pancake can have a savoury or a sweet filling. A speciality is to top the galette with ham and an egg. The egg is swirled over, breaking the yolk into the white, and cooked until just set. The pancake is folded and served at once. Galettes are sometimes found in other parts of France.

◆◆ Galette de la Chaise-Dieu
Not a pancake but a cheese which comes from Auvergne. Unusually for this area, it is made from goats' milk and is very slightly sweet.

Gamba
Large prawn.

◆◆ Gaperon
Garlic-flavoured, rounded cheese from Auvergne, made from cows' milk.

◆◆◆ Garbure
A soup or stew made from mixed vegetables, mainly root ones, with bacon. Originating in Gascony, it is found all over France.

Gâteau
Sponge cake or tart, sweet or sometimes savoury.

◆ Gâteau au fromage
Cheesecake. Although the French do not have a passion for this particular dessert, it is becoming increasingly popular.

Gaufre, gaufrette
Wafer biscuit or waffle.

Gelée, en
In aspic.

Genièvre
Juniper. The berries are used in

many savoury dishes from the Ardennes, and some aperitifs too.

Génoise
Sponge cake.

◆◆ Gex, bleu de
A firm blue-veined cows' milk cheese of flat cylindrical shape which comes from the Haut-Jura. Once made in huts on the mountain slopes, it is now manufactured in modern dairies.

Gibier
Game.

◆◆ Gien
A cows' milk cheese from the Loire valley, cured in wood ash.

◆ Gigoret
Pig's head cooked in blood and red wine, a dish from Poitou-Charentes.

Gigot
Leg of lamb, occasionally goat.

◆◆◆ Gigot pourri
Lamb cooked with whole cloves of garlic, a dish from Rouergue.

Gingembre
Ginger.

Gîte à la noix.
Beef silverside.

Glace
Ice, ice-cream.

Glace au café
Coffee ice-cream, as opposed to *café glacé*, iced coffee.

◆ Gouda Français
Gouda type cheese is made in France as well as in Holland, although it tastes slightly milder. There is also a French Edam. Both are made in the area along the Belgian border.

◆◆◆ Gougère
A delicious light cheese-flavoured choux pastry bun or ring from Burgundy.

Goujons
Small strips of fish, coated in breadcrumbs and deep fried.

Gourmandise
Sweetmeat.

◆ Gournay
A well-known cows' milk cheese from the town of that name in Normandy. It is soft, salty and comes in a flat disc shape.

Goûter
To taste.

Goyave
Guava.

Grain de cassis
Blackcurrant.

Vegetables of summer

Granité
Type of crunchy water ice.
Grappe de raisins
Bunch of grapes.
Gratin
A dish with a crust of browned breadcrumbs, possibly mixed with cheese.
◆◆ **Gratin dauphinois**
Potato slices baked in milk and sometimes cheese (see recipe pages 100–1).
Gratterons
Fried cubed pork and pork fat.
◆◆ **Grecque, à la**
Southern vegetable dish of mushrooms, aubergines or others, poached in oil and herbs, served hot or cold.
Grenade
Pomegranate.
Grenadin
Thick slice of veal; the term is sometimes applied to other meat.
◆ **Grignaudes**
Fried pieces of pork, from Berry. Rather like RILLONS, usually eaten cold.
Gril, sur le
Grilled.
Grillade
Grill, of steak, lamb chop, etc.
◆◆◆ **Grillade au fenouil**
Fish, usually mullet or sea bass, grilled over sprigs of fennel often over a barbecue, a dish of Provence.
◆ **Gris de Lille**
A very salty, strong smelling cheese from the north of France. Made from cows' milk, it is recognisable by its distinctive square shape.
Grive
Thrush, now banned as food under EC regulations. Sometimes still found as canned pâté.
Gros mollet
Lumpfish.
Groseille
Redcurrant, white currant.
Groseille à maquereau
Gooseberry.
Groseille de cheval
Cranberry.
◆◆ **Gruyère**
Both the French and the Swiss lay claim to this cheese and, under a court decision made in 1951, both countries are allowed to call their product by this name. The two best known French versions are *Gruyère de Comté*, made in the Franche-Comté region, and *Beaufort* which has no holes in it. (The French also make EMMENTHAL, which used to be considered a type of Gruyère but is now classed as a separate cheese.)

H

◆ **Hachis parmentier**
The French equivalent of shepherd's pie: minced lamb topped with mashed potato.
◆◆ **Halicot** or **haricot de mouton**
Stewed mutton with root vegetables but rarely haricot beans.
Hareng
Herring.
Harissa
A fiery paste of red chillies and spices. Buy it in tubes or jars to serve with COUSCOUS.
◆◆ **Hochepot**
A filling soup of beef, mutton, salt pork, pigs' ears and tail, cabbage and root vegetables.
◆◆◆ **Hollandaise**
Hot or warm sauce made from

butter, wine and lemon juice, thickened with egg yolks.

Homard
Lobster.

◆◆◆ Homard à l'armoricaine/ l'américaine
Lobster served with a sauce of brandy, white wine, onions, tomatoes and herbs. A dish which comes from Brittany and is found mainly in the north of France.

◆ Homard thermidor
Sautéed lobster cooked in a creamy white wine sauce, topped with Parmesan cheese then browned under the grill.

Hors d'oeuvre
Mixture (usually cold) of meat, fish and vegetable dishes served as an appetiser.

Huître
Oyster.

I

◆◆ Igny
A mild disc-shaped cheese from the Champagne area. It is made from cows' milk by the monks at the Abbey of Igny in the Marne district.

◆◆ Ile flottante
A favourite French pudding, islands of egg white poached in (and floating in) custard. The same name is occasionally given to a type of custard trifle.

Indienne, à l'
With a curry-flavoured sauce, usually a mild one.

◆ Iraty
A strong cheese containing a mix of cows' and ewes' milk from the Basque country. The cheese varies in its pungency from season to season,

Atlantic oyster farm

according to how much ewes' milk is included.

Italienne, à l'
Served with pasta, mushrooms, tomato.

J

Jambon, jambonneau
Ham.

◆◆ Jonchée
Delicious fresh cream cheese from Poitou-Charentes. The name is also used in other parts of France – the Loire and Brittany for instance – for a type of junket.

Joue
Cheek, usually of pork.

Julienne
Thin strips of vegetables, sometimes poached in butter,

Ham: Regional Specialities
Many different parts of France have their own special hams – from the area around Toulouse, for instance, from the Jura, from Morlaix in Brittany and from the Ardennes. The most famous ham of all is probably the mild cured *Jambon de Bayonne*, which is sold all over France. *Jambon cru* is raw, often wind-dried, ham. *Jambon de York* is a name for ordinary ham. *Jambon fumé* is smoked ham.

◆◆ **Jambon persillé** Ham that is usually cubed, then preserved Bourgogne style with parsley in a type of wine jelly.

Jambonneau A small ham, usually a knuckle bone.

◆◆ **Jambonnette** Dry salt pork sausage shaped to look like a ham, which comes from the Vivarais area.

Country ham

served as a garnish for a main dish.

Jus
Juice, gravy.

L

◆◆◆ **Laguiole**
One of the great AOC cheeses from the Aubrac area. It has a strong herb flavour as it is made with milk from cows raised on land with thyme, fennel and other pungent plants growing on it.

Lait
Milk.

Laitue
Lettuce.

◆◆◆ **Landaise, à la**
Cooked in goose fat with garlic and pine kernels, from the Landes area in the southwest.

Langouste
Spiny lobster, sea crayfish.

Langoustine
Dublin bay prawn, large scampi.

◆ **Langres**
A disc-shaped cheese from Champagne or a cone-shaped soft version from Burgundy, made from cows' milk.

Langue or **languette**
Tongue.

Langue de chat
Long thin biscuit.

Languier
Smoked pork tongue.

Lapin or **lapereau**
Rabbit.

◆ **Laqueuille, bleu de**
A strong, soft blue cheese, very like ROQUEFORT, from Auvergne.

◆ Laruns
A cheese made from ewes' milk which comes from the Basque country.

◆◆ Laums
A loaf-shaped cheese made from cows' milk from the Burgundy/Franche-Comté area, often soaked in coffee.

Lentille
Lentil.

◆ Levroux
A strong-smelling but mild cheese from the Loire made from goats' milk, similar to VALENÇAY.

Lièvre
Hare. *Civet de lièvre* is jugged hare.

◆ Ligueil
A cylindrical goats' milk cheese from the Loire valley with a strong flavour.

Limande
Dab (fish).

Limon
Lime.

◆◆ Livarot
Small, brown, pungent, cylindrical-shaped cheese from Normandy, made from cows' milk.

◆ Lormes
A cone-shaped goats' milk cheese from Nivernais.

Lotte de mer
Monkfish.

◆ Loudes, bleu de
Yet another blue-veined cheese from the Massif Central. This one, which is made from cows' milk, comes from the Le Puy area.

◆◆ Loukinka
Spicy garlic sausage from the Basque country.

◆◆◆ Loup de mer
Sea bass. Served in the south of France grilled on fennel twigs, often flamed in Pernod (*loup grillé au fenouil*).

◆ Lusignan
A fresh cheese from the Poitou area made from goats' milk, sometimes used in cheesecakes.

◆◆◆ Lyonnaise, à la
Cooked with onions, Lyon style. This usually refers to potatoes, sometimes liver.

M

Macedoine
Mixture of diced fruit or vegetables, used either in a salad or *hors d'oeuvre* or as a dessert.

Mâche
Corn salad, lamb's lettuce. A small-leafed, winter variety of lettuce with tender dark green leaves that have a fairly unexciting lettuce flavour.

Madeleine
Small conical sponge cake.

◆ Magnum
A rich, creamy disc-shaped cheese from Normandy, similar to BRILLAT-SAVARIN.

Maigre
Lean.

◆◆ Maigret/magret
Grilled sliced breast of duck served pink and rare.

Maïs
Sweetcorn.

Mange-tout
Small pods with undeveloped peas in them, eaten whole.

Maquereau
Mackerel.

◆ Maquereau au vin blanc
Mackerel cooked in white wine. Often served cold as a first course in northern France.

◆◆◆ Marbrade
Pig's head in aspic, a dish from southwest France.
Marcassin
Young wild boar.
◆◆ Marchand de vin
Meat, usually steak, with red wine, and shallots.
◆◆ Marmande farci
The giant beefsteak tomato of the south, stuffed either with a mix of chopped cooked tuna, onion and olive oil, or minced lamb and onion. A very attractive starter.
◆◆◆ Maroilles
One of the AOC cheeses of France which comes from the edge of the Ardennes. It is also one of the oldest cheeses, said to have been invented by monks at the abbey there over a thousand years ago. Do not be put off by its pungent smell; it tastes delicious if a trifle spicy. Often used in *tartes* in the north of France.
Marron
Chestnut.
◆◆ Marron Mont-Blanc
Chestnut purée pushed through a sieve or mincer and topped with whipped cream to resemble the mountain – Europe's highest.
Marrons glacés
Chestnuts preserved and glazed in sugar.
Massepain
Marzipan, or sometimes a cake made with almond paste.
◆ Matefaim
Type of thick pancake or batter pudding from Berry. It can be sweet or savoury.
◆ Matelote
Casserole of freshwater fish with onions, mushrooms and wine.
◆◆ Méchoui
Barbecued lamb, North African style, often with cumin. Found in Paris or in the south – anywhere where there is an Arab population of any size.
Médaillon
Small round fillet steak.
Mélange
Blend or mixture.
Menthe
Mint, mint flavoured.
◆◆◆ Merguez
A popular spicy raw sausage of Spanish origins.
Merlan
Whiting.
Merluche
Hake, salted or fresh.
◆ Mesclun
Mixed green salad from Provence. Now sold bagged in supermarkets.
◆ Metton, mettons
A type of cheese spread made from heated whey. Sometimes served on croûtons of toasted bread, a dish from the Jura.
◆ Meunière, à la
Flour-coated and fried or grilled with butter, lemon juice and parsley.
Mignonnette
Small round fillet of lamb.
◆ Mignot
A Normandy cheese very similar to the famous LIVAROT.
◆ Mille-feuille
Flaky pastry slices sandwiched with jam and cream.
Minute
Flash-cooked steak or sometimes sole, grilled or fried.
Mirabelle
Small yellow plum.
Mirepoix
Diced root vegetable and bacon mix, cooked in butter. It forms the basis of several sauces.

Café life, French style

◆ Mirliton
Little pastry cakes featuring ground almonds, from Normandy.

◆ Miroton
Cooked meat, usually beef, with onions and mustard-flavoured sauce. A dish for using up leftover roast or boiled beef.

◆ Mode, à la
Marinated meat, usually beef, braised in wine with calf's foot, bacon, vegetables.

Mollet
Soft, soft-boiled, as for eggs.

◆ Monsieur
A firm and fruity Normandy cheese made from cows' milk. It has a red-spotted rind and a strong smell.

◆◆ Montoire
A mild goats' milk cheese with a delicious taste from the Loire Valley.

◆ Montrachet
A creamy cylindrical goats' milk cheese, sold wrapped in chestnut, or sometimes vine, leaves.

◆ Montségur
A cows' milk cheese from Languedoc–Roussillon with a very mild, bland flavour.

◆◆ Morbier
A strong-flavoured cows' milk cheese from the Jura. Easily identified because it has a black streak of soot running through the centre.

Morceau
Small morcel, tiny portion.

Morille/morel
A type of wild mushroom which is rare and expensive. Dark brown to black, with a honeycomb-textured cap, this needs thorough washing and long cooking. They are springtime mushrooms; also sold dried. Pale morels are cheaper because they do not have as good a flavour.

Mornay
With a cheese sauce.

Morue
Cod, sometimes dried or more

usually salted. Used to make BRANDADE.

Moules
Mussels. *Moules farcies* are stuffed mussels.

◆◆◆ Moules à la marinière
Mussels cooked in a thin onion and white wine sauce.

Mousse
Light mixture, type of cold soufflé.

Mousseline
With whipped cream or egg white.

Moutarde
Mustard.

Mouton
Mutton.

◆◆ Munster
One of France's AOC cheeses, a pungent disc-shaped cheese with a dark red skin from Alsace. It looks soft and mild but has a very strong flavour and smell, and is something of an acquired taste. You will sometimes find it sold with a cumin seed flavouring which gives it an aniseed tang.

Mûre
Mulberry.

Mûre de ronce
Blackberry.

◆ Murol
A mild cows' milk cheese from the area of that name in the Dordogne. It is similar in flavour to the better known SAINT-NECTAIRE.

Myrtille
Bilberry.

Walnut and chocolate cakes from the Dordogne, a nut-growing area

N

◆◆ Nantua
A fish dish from Normandy or Brittany, often sole, served garnished with crayfish tails.

Nature
Plain, eg *omelette nature*. The term is also used to refer to coffee or tea, served without milk.

◆ Navarin
A simple lamb stew with onions and potatoes.

Navet
Turnip.

◆◆ Négresse en chemise
A very popular French pudding of chocolate ice-cream or mousse served like a sandcastle, with a 'moat' of cream round the edge.

◆◆◆ Neufchâtel
One of the great AOC cheeses called after the town of that name in Normandy. Usually sold or served on a bed of straw, it

comes in many shapes from cylindrical to heart-shaped. You may also find it sold under the name of *Bondon*. It has a white rind and a soft texture and flavour.

◆◆ Niçoise, à la
Nice fashion, usually a dish that relies heavily on tomatoes, garlic, anchovies, olives and, probably, aubergines.

Noisette
Nut, hazelnut. Sometimes a small cake topped with hazelnuts.

Noisette/noix d'agneau, boeuf veau
A small round cut of meat – lamb, beef, veal.

Noix
Nut, walnut.

◆◆◆ Normande, à la
Meat or poultry cooked Normandy style with apples, cream and cider or CALVADOS. If it refers to fish, it is usually with a simple white wine and cream sauce.

◆ Nougat
Soft chewy sweet containing nuts and honey from Montélimar. Although nougat is now made everywhere, Montélimar is renowned for this confection and it is worth taking some home. Usually sold cut in squares or bars.

Nouilles
Noodles.

Nouvelle cuisine
This style of food preparation and cooking was promoted and made popular in the seventies. *Nouvelle cuisine* was based on simple, light cooking methods applied to the freshest of ingredients. Complicated methods and combinations, rich sauces and large portions were replaced by carefully selected foods served with minimal additional flavouring. This evolved into dishes served in tiny portions with more emphasis on artistic presentation than on providing a well-balanced meal. Now rather passé.

O

Oeuf
Egg. *Oeuf brouillé* is scrambled egg, *oeuf à la coque* is an egg that is soft-boiled in its shell. Hard boiled egg is *oeuf dur* and *oeuf en cocotte* is egg cooked in a small ramekin. *Oeuf frit* or *oeuf à la poêle* means fried egg, while *oeuf mollet* is an egg that is soft boiled and shelled. Poached egg is *oeuf poché* and *oeuf sur le plat* is baked in butter.

Oie/oison
Goose, a favourite choice on the menu in the Dordogne/Landes area of France, also in Alsace.

Oignon
Onion.

◆◆ Oiseau sans tête
Not a small headless bird, as you might imagine, but stuffed rolled fillet of beef.

◆ Oléron
A cheese from the Ile d'Oléron district on the Atlantic coast, made, as are many cheeses in this area, from ewes' milk. Of no particular shape, it has a mild creamy flavour.

Olive
Olive. Most French olives are grown in Provence. Green olives are unripe and black ones ripe fruit. The wrinkled ones have been left on the trees a long time before picking.

Olives are usually preserved in brine and may be garlic flavoured or stuffed with pimento or nuts.

Olivet bleu
A blue-veined cheese from the Orléans area made from cows' milk and matured in caves. It has a pleasant, fairly mild taste.

◆ Olivet cendré
A similar cheese to OLIVET BLEU, from the same area. Cured in wood ash, it has a slightly firmer flavour.

Omelette
Omelette. Served in both sweet and savoury ways in France.

Ordinaire
Ordinary, straight. *Vin ordinaire*, for instance, is a simple local wine.

An Omelette: A French Culinary Treat
Eating a good omelette is to experience classic, simple cooking at its best. Perhaps with a salad, or some bread, it should be a meal to remember.
Omelette au jambon is an omelette with ham. *Omelette aux champignons* is a mushroom omelette, *aux fines herbes* is one with finely chopped herbs stirred in. *Omelette au fromage* is a cheese omelette, while *omelette nature* is a plain omelette. *A la confiture* is a sweet fluffy omelette with jam.
The phrase: 'I'll just have an omelette', does not apply in France: if you order one it will almost certainly contain at least four eggs.

Oreille or **oreillette**
Ear of pig, used quite often in country dishes.

◆◆ Orrys, les
A mountain cheese from the Languedoc–Roussillon area, made from cows' milk. It is hard in texture and strong tasting, and comes in large flat discs. Often used in place of Parmesan for grating over food.

Os, à l'
With bone marrow, which is used for flavouring sauces and stews.

◆◆ Ouillade
Pungent garlic-flavoured bean and vegetable soup from the Languedoc area.

Oursin
Sea urchin. Frequently found in dishes of seafood.

P

Paillette dorée
Cheese straw.

Paillettes d'oignons frits
Fried crisp onion rings.

Pain
Bread. For more information on the variety of breads see page 87.

◆◆ Pain au chocolat
Rectangular croissant with chocolate in the middle. Eaten warm.

Palombe
Woodpigeon.

Palourde
Cockle or clam.

Pamplemousse
Grapefruit.

◆◆ Pan bagna, bagnat
Salad sandwich from Provence with tomatoes or other salad ingredients, olives and

Fresh bread daily, a way of life

anchovies moistened with olive oil.

Panaché
Mixed, as in *salade panachée.*

Panais
Parsnip.

Papillotte, en
Meat or fish cooked and served in a little packet of greased paper or foil.

Parfait
Frozen mousse or mousse-like cream, used in desserts, with a chocolate, vanilla or strawberry flavour.

Parmentier
A dish which contains potatoes. *Potage parmentier* is very similar to VICHYSSOISE, but is a slightly less elegant leek and potato soup.

◆◆ Passe-l'an
A hard cheese from Languedoc which, as its name implies (passed the year), is left to mature for at least one year – probably two. It is sold in segments from enormous flat discs, and is often grated over food.

Patate
Sweet potato.

Pâte
This word can mean either pastry or pasta, according to what is associated with it. *Pâte brisée* is shortcrust pastry, *pâte à chou* is choux pastry, and *pâte feuilletée* is flaky or puff pastry. The French also have *pâte sablée* which is a form of rich shortcrust with sugar in it, used for *tartes. Pâte d'amandes* is marzipan and *pâte frollée* is almond flavoured pastry.

Pâte de fruits
A fruit jelly.

Pâté
A cooked meat or fish paste which can be smooth or chunky, served cold.

◆◆◆ Pâté de campagne
Coarse pâté, usually made from pork and almost certainly including garlic and other herbs.

◆◆ Pâté de foie gras
Expensive goose liver pâté,

Sweet peas: petits pois

sometimes laced with truffles, which you can often buy canned.

◆ Pâté en croûte
Pâté cooked in a pastry covering, rather like a game pie.

◆◆◆ Pâté maison
This pâté is likely to be smooth and based on chicken or pig's liver.

Paupiette
Slice of meat, such as veal or beef, occasionally fish, which is rolled round a savoury filling.

◆ Pavé d'Auge
A Normandy cheese with a strong taste yet a soft texture. It comes in squares and is golden yellow in colour.

Pavés
Gingerbread.

Pays, de
Of the region.

Pêche
Peach.

◆ Pêche Melba
Peach on ice-cream with raspberry purée.

◆ Pélardons
A family of small soft goats' milk cheeses from Cévennes. The name is also given to small cheeses cured in MARC (local brandy), found in the Savoie region.

Perche
Freshwater perch.

Perdreau/perdrix
Partridge.

Persil
Parsley.

Persillé
With parsley, or parsley sauce.

◆ Persillé
Name of a series of blue cheeses from Savoie made from goats' milk. Names to look for are *persillé d'Aravis, persillé de Thônes* or *persillé du Grand-Bornand* – they are all basically the same cheese.

◆◆ Pet de nonne
Literally 'nun's fart', this is the local name in Burgundy for a light soufflé fritter, similar to a *beignet.*

◆ Peteram
Sheep's trotter and tripe stew from Languedoc. To be avoided by those who are timid about eating offal.

Petit beurre
Small biscuit, made from butter.

◆◆◆ Petit Bressan
A delightful small cheese from Lyonnais. It is made from either cows' or goats' milk, or a mixture of the two.

Petit four
Small after-dinner cake or biscuit, usually served with coffee.

◆◆ Petit-Suisse
A famous brand name for tiny round cream cheeses which come from nowhere near Switzerland but from Normandy. The cheese is so soft that you can eat it with a spoon, and people sometimes sprinkle sugar over it before eating.

Petites
Tripe of sheep or veal from Languedoc.

Petits pois
Small sweet peas. Often served with baby cocktail-size onions. Very good bought canned.

◆ Picodon
Generic name for a series of goats' milk cheeses from the Drôme–Rhône Valley area.

Pièce de boeuf
Prime cut of beef.

Pied
Trotter, foot.

◆◆◆ Pieds et paquets
Sheep tripe folded into packets, cooked with trotters, tomatoes and wine; a well-known Provençal dish which is unexpectedly delicious.

Pigeon/pigeonneau
Pigeon.

Pignons
Pine nuts. These are used a great deal in Provençal cooking – in *soupe au pistou* for instance, and in some dishes from the Landes area.

◆ Pigouille
A creamy cheese from Charentais, near the Atlantic coast. It can be made from cows', goats' or ewes' milk and is usually sold wrapped in straw.

Piment
Green or red pepper.

Piment doux
Sweet pepper.

Piment fort
Chilli, cayenne.

Pintade/pintadeau
Guinea fowl.

◆◆ Pipérade
An egg dish which comes from the Basque country with onions, red peppers and tomatoes (see recipe pages 101–2).

◆◆ Pissaladière
Type of yeast-dough tart, similar to pizza, covered with anchovies, olives and tomatoes. Found everywhere in the South of France.

Pissenlit
Dandelion. The phrase literally means wet-the-bed. Dandelion leaves are used in salads, particularly with a combination of other wild leaves.

◆◆◆ Pistou
A sauce based on basil pounded with garlic, pine nuts and olive oil. Used, among other dishes, to flavour a Provençal soup. Similar to Italian pesto.

◆◆◆ Pithiviers
Well-known, delicious flaky pastry gâteau, filled with FRANGIPANE (almond cream) and drowned in rum. Named after a town in Orléanais where it is served as a speciality.

◆ Pithiviers au foin
Not a pastry but a soft disc-shaped cheese from the Loire area, sold covered with strips of dried grass.

Planche de charcuterie
A platter of cold meats.

Plateau de fromages
Cheeseboard, assortment of cheeses. In France they will certainly be fresh and there should be a good selection of local ones.

◆◆◆ Plateau de fruits de mer
Platter of seafood, usually laid

out decoratively, garnished with seaweed. The best *plateaux* come from Normandy and Brittany.

Plie
Plaice.

◆◆ Pochade
Stew of freshwater fish with raisins and carrots, from Savoie.

Poché
Poached.

Point, à
Medium done, eg steak.

Pointe
Tip; for example *pointe d'asperge* (asparagus tip).

Poire
Pear.

Poire de terre
Jerusalem artichoke.

Poireau
Leek.

Poirée
White beet, chard.

◆◆ Poires Alma
Pears cooked in port.

◆ Poires Belle-Hélène
Cooked pears with ice-cream and hot chocolate sauce.

Pois
Peas. *Petits pois* are little sweet green peas.

Pois chiches
Chick-peas. Used in dishes in the south.

Poisson
Fish.

Poisson volant
Flying fish.

Poitrine
Breast of lamb or veal.

◆◆ Poivre d'ane
A goats' milk cheese, well worth looking out for, from the hinterland of the Côte d'Azur. It has a distinctive herby flavour.

Pomme
Apple.

Pomme de terre
Potato. The words *de terre* are usually dispensed with, leaving it to your good sense to decide whether it is apple or potato you are getting.

◆◆ Pont-l'Evêque
Famous cows' milk cheese from Normandy which comes from the town of that name. It is rectangular in shape and has a relatively mild taste.

Porc
Pork. A cornerstone of French

Lively shopping at the market

Potatoes: Cooked in a Variety of Classic Dishes
France is, of course, the place to sample many of the famous classic potato dishes at their best. However, for plain cooked potatoes order *pommes à l'anglaise*. If you want potatoes baked in their jackets ask for them *en robe de chambre*. New potatoes cooked slowly in butter over a gentle heat are *pommes fondantes* – golden, soft and delicious. Simple steamed potatoes are *pommes au vapeur*.
Pommes allumettes Thin cut chips.
Pommes Anna A dish of thinly sliced potatoes, oven-baked in butter.
Pommes dauphinoises Somewhat similar to *pommes Anna* but moister – the potatoes are sliced, then oven-baked in milk.
Pommes duchesse Puréed potato piped decoratively on the plate.
Pommes frites, frites Chips.
Pommes Lyonnais A delicious dish of potatoes sautéed with onion.
Pommes mousseline Soufflé potatoes – sometimes puréed with beaten egg white, nowadays more often with cream.
Pommes paillées Straw thin, matchstick-like chips.
Pommes rissolées Small round potatoes, deep fried.

cuisine, pork appears in a huge range of dishes and, of course, in the charcuterie where, it is claimed, every part of the pig is used except the squeak. *Fromage de porc* is a rather confusing name which means brawn.

◆ **Porc, pré-salé de**
Pieces of pork cooked in brine.

◆ **Porché**
Stewed pigs' ears and feet, from Brittany.

◆◆ **Port-Salut**
A mild cows' milk cheese from Brittany, very similar to SAINT-PAULIN in taste.

Pot, au
Cooked in a pot, usually boiled.

Potage
Soup. In general, it is lighter than its counterpart, SOUPE.

◆◆ **Potage bonne femme**
A leek and potato soup not unlike VICHYSSOISE.

◆◆ **Potage Crécy**
Carrot soup.

◆◆ **Potage parmentier**
A potato-based soup, usually with leeks added.

◆ **Potage paysanne**
A straightforward mixed vegetable soup.

◆◆◆ **Pot-au-feu**
A traditional French dish, a hearty mix of boiled beef, with carrots, leeks, turnips and potatoes. Originally from southwest France, it is likely to be found everywhere. There are even *pot-au-feu* stock cubes available.

◆◆ **Potée**
A thick soup of bacon, cabbage and potatoes.

Potiron
Pumpkin. Used often in France for soups.

Poulet, poularde, poulette
Various names for chicken.

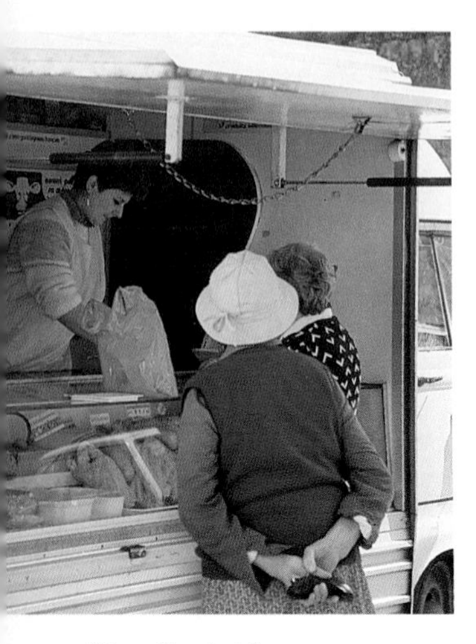

A travelling butcher

◆◆◆ Poulet à estragon
Chicken with tarragon (see recipe on pages 106-7).

◆◆◆ Poulet au vinaigre
Chicken cooked with shallots, wine vinegar and cream from Lyonnais, a very tasty dish. (Vinegar is quite often used in French cooking in place of wine.)

◆◆ Poulet Marengo
Chicken cooked with garlic, mushrooms and tomatoes.

◆◆ Poulpe
Octopus. *Poulpe frit*, fried and crisp; otherwise stewed, perhaps *à la provençale* with onions, garlic and tomatoes.

◆◆ Pourly
Small cylindrical goats' milk cheese from Burgundy. It is a good choice for children because of its mild flavour.

Poussin
Baby chicken.

Pouvron
Sweet pepper.

Praire
Clam.

Praliné(e)
Caramelised or covered with crushed toffee.

◆◆ Printanière, à la
Referring to spring. A dish, often lamb, accompanied by young mixed vegetables tossed in butter.

◆◆ Profiteroles
Choux pastry buns filled with cream, sometimes topped with chocolate sauce (*au chocolat*).

◆◆ Provençal
Cooked the traditional Provençal way, usually with oil, tomatoes, peppers, garlic, anchovies.

Prune
Plum, not prune – see below.

Pruneau
Prune.

Q

◆◆ Quenelle
Boat-shaped mousse of puréed fish or white meat poached in liquid; for example *quenelles de brochet* (pike). *Quenelles* are found in restaurants all over France. They are shaped using two spoons and poached to turn out rather like very light dumplings. However, the same mixture may be set in a mould to cook in a *bain marie* (a container of water). In kitchenware shops, you can buy little tin moulds for making *quenelles* yourself.

◆◆ Quercy, bleu du
A blue-veined cheese from the area around Figeac which tastes very much like the better known BLEU D'AUVERGNE.

Quetsch
Plum. Plums are also called *prunes*, while the prune itself is *pruneau*.

Queue
Tail.

Queue de boeuf
Oxtail.

◆◆ **Quiche**
Savoury egg custard-filled pastry flan. There are many varieties of quiche. Miniature ones are often served as AMUSE-GUEULES – appetisers before a meal in the more expensive restaurants.

◆◆ **Quiche Lorraine**
The classic quiche, with diced bacon and cream, which comes from Lorraine.

R

◆ **Rabot**
Whole apple cooked in pastry. A popular dessert from Champagne.

Racine
Root vegetable – turnip, carrot, and so on. The word *racine* means root.

Radis
Radish.

Ragoût
A stew, usually a hearty one, prepared peasant style.

◆◆ **Raie**
Ray or skate. Often served simply, cooked in butter.

Raifort
Horseradish.

Raisin
Grape. The word *grappe*, which people sometimes use by mistake, means a bunch of something, not necessarily grapes.

Ramequin
Small individual pot, used mainly for baking an egg or egg and cheese dishes.

Ramereau or **ramier**
Woodpigeon.

Râpé
Grated. In the supermarkets you will often find packs of ready-grated cheese, such as Gruyère, and grated carrot for salads.

◆◆ **Râpée**
Thick grated potato pancake, like Swiss rösti, which comes from Lyonnais. The raw potato is coarsely grated into a pan of foaming butter and oil, cooked on one side, then turned over.

◆◆◆ **Ratatouille**
Provençal dish of aubergines, peppers, tomatoes, courgettes and garlic, cooked in olive oil. It is usually served as a side dish, but makes a good lunch dish if you are self-catering. Ratatouille is delicious served hot or cold, with chunks of French bread (see recipe pages 102–3).

Rave
Turnip.

Rave céleri
Celeriac.

◆ **Ravigote**
Seasoned brown shallot sauce.

◆ **Reblochon**
A mild AOC cheese from Savoie. It is made from cows' milk and has a creamy taste.

Réchauffé
Reheated, made with cooked meat.

Reine, à la
With chicken.

Reine-Claude
Greengage. A very popular fruit in France, grown widely in the Dordogne.

◆◆ Rémoulade
Mayonnaise seasoned with mustard and herbs, capers or gherkins. Often served spooned over shredded celeriac.

◆ Riceys, les
A cows' milk cheese that comes from the Troyes area, south of Champagne, It has a soft texture and comes in flat discs covered in wood ash.

◆ Rigotte
A typical cylindrical goats' milk cheese from Ardèche, sold under the name of *rigotte de Condrieu* or *rigotte de Pelusin*.

◆◆ Rillettes
Potted minced or cubed pork, occasionally goose or even rabbit, slow-cooked for a long time, then shredded. Tasting rather like old-fashioned meat paste, they are usually served spread on bread. Not as savoury as pâté but very similar in appearance. You will find them on the menu all over central France.

◆◆ Rillons
Crisp pieces of cooked pork or goose, browned and preserved in fat. The name is probably a contraction of *grillon*. Rillons have a very different texture to RILLETTES with which they are often confused. Buy them from the *charcuterie*.

Ris
Veal or lamb sweetbreads. Many people make the mistake of misreading the menu, and think that they have ordered rice (*riz*) instead.

Rissole
Deep-fried fritter, meatball. It can occasionally turn out to be a ball of vegetables or fish.

Rissolé
Baked brown, fried.

Riz
Rice. *Riz au blanc* is plain white boiled rice and *riz au gras* is fried rice.

◆ Rogeret des Cévennes
A goats' milk cheese with a colourful rind. It is very similar to PÉLARDON, from the same area.

Rognon
Kidney. Used in a number of French dishes.

◆ Rognons Turbigo
Popular kidney dish with sausages, mushrooms, white wine and tomato sauce.

Romarin
Rosemary.

Rond de gigot
Thick slice of leg of mutton.

◆◆◆ Roquefort
Probably the most popular blue-veined cheese in France, with an AOC rating. It is made from ewes' milk in Cévennes. Roquefort is matured for three months or more in the caves of Roquefort-sur-Soulzon before being sold. It has a very salty taste and a crumbly texture, and can be found wrapped in convenient wedge-shaped packs in supermarkets.

◆ Rosbif
Roast beef. In France if you see this on the menu, it is usually served very rare, sliced and cold, possibly as part of an ASSIETTE ANGLAISE – a plate of cold cooked meats.

Rôti
Roasted.

Rouget
Red mullet.

◆◆◆ Rouille
A hot, garlicky sauce in which soaked bread is mixed with garlic and paprika or cayenne pepper, sometimes canned

sweet red pepper. An essential accompaniment, served spread on slices of French bread, to fish soups in Provence (see recipe page 99).

Roulade
Rolled and stuffed, usually meat, sometimes fish or an omelette.

Roulé
Sweet or savoury roll

◆ **Rouy**
A soft cheese made from cows' milk which is manufactured in Dijon and sold in square boxes. It has a powerful smell.

◆◆ **Ruffec**
A disc-shaped cheese from Charentais. It is made from goats' milk, as most cheeses from this area are, but it has a fuller taste than most of them.

Rutabaga
Swede.

S

◆◆ **Sabayon**
Dessert made from egg yolks, sugar and wine. Similar to Italian *zabaione* (or *zabaglione*) and sometimes served as a sauce.

◆◆ **Saint-Benoît**
Saint-Benoist. A round fruity cheese from the Loire, made from cows' milk, which is well worth trying.

◆ **Saint-Florentin**
Another round cheese, this time from Burgundy. It is made from cows' milk, has a distinctive brownish red rind and a full taste.

◆ **Saint-Gildas-des-Bois**
A rich triple-cream cheese from Brittany made with cows' milk. It has a rather mouldy smell.

◆◆ **Saint-Honoré**
Gâteau of choux pastry and confectioner's custard.

◆ **Saint-Marcellin, Tomme de Saint-Marcellin**
A mild cheese from Savoie, made from cows' milk.

◆◆ **Saint-Nectaire**
Hardish cheese from the Dordogne, made from cows' milk and sold in large wheels. It has an AOC rating, and smells rather mildewy – not surprisingly since it is usually ripened in local caves.

◆◆ **Saint-Paulin**
A type of round cheese with a

Café in the spa town of Vittel

distinctive orange rind, made from cows' milk all over the north of France. It is fairly hard and mild, and tastes like PORT-SALUT.

◆◆ Saint-Rémy
A strong smelling cheese from Lorraine with a spicy taste. It is made from cows' milk, has a reddish rind and a square shape.

◆ Sainte-Foy, bleu de Sainte-Foy
A blue-veined cheese from Savoie made from cows' milk. It has a strong taste.

◆ Sainte-Maure
A strong-smelling and tasting goats' milk cheese from the Loire. It is cylindrical and has a distinctive stick of straw running through the centre.

Salade
Salad.

◆ Salaison
Salted meat or fish hors d'oeuvres with anchovies, olives, etc.

Salé
Salted.

Salé, petit
Small pieces of salt pork.

◆◆ Salmis
Game casserole, where the meat is first roasted then finished in wine sauce; rather similar to braised dishes.

◆◆ Salpicon
An old French word for fish or meat with diced vegetables in

Salad: Simple or Sophisticated

The most simple, classic French salad consists of only fresh, perfect lettuce, torn by hand and served with an oil and vinegar dressing.

A *salade simple* is a plain salad. A *salade composée* is a substantial mixed salad with eggs, beans, ie something fairly hearty, in it. *Salade panachée* is an ordinary mixed salad. A green salad is a *salade verte*. You may be asked if you want it *avec* or *sans l'ail* – with or without garlic.

Salade de fruits Fruit salad.

◆◆◆ Salade niçoise Salad, from Nice, of tomatoes, peppers, French beans, olives, anchovies and eggs. It varies in size, depending on whether it is served as a starter or a main dish. Tuna is often added for a more substantial salad (see recipe pages 99–100).

◆ Salade Russe Russian salad of diced root vegetables in mayonnaise.

Saladier Large mixed salad.

Salad with maigret de canard

one of a variety of sauces or, if cold, with a mayonnaise. The result is used as a rather rarified stuffing. Often used to fill little pastry *barquettes* for appetisers or hors d'oeuvres.

Salsifis
Salsify, the oyster plant. It is either served young, eaten raw in a salad or cooked with a béchamel sauce. Scorzonera is a root vegetable closely related to salsify. Salsify is a white root, scorzonera is a black root.

◆◆ Sandwich
Roll or piece of long loaf, often filled with ham. A French sandwich made with a split *ficelle* or a baton loaf, stuffed full of pâté and salad, makes a meal in itself. It is easy to assemble and ideal to eat in the car if you are travelling. A more elegant version can be made by using a BRIOCHE filled with *pâté de foie gras* – easier on the teeth too.

◆ Sanglier
Wild boar. It has a gamey taste that does not bear much resemblance to home-produced pork. You will find that wild boar features quite frequently on the menu in the countryside. Wild boar pâté is considered to be a delicacy. You can find it on sale in mountainous places as far south as Sault in Provence. However, its taste is a little disappointing, and its cost expensive, so try it before you buy a jar or two to take home.

◆ Sassenage
A blue-veined cheese from Savoie, usually made from a mix of cows' and goats' milk.

Saucisse
Sausage.

Saumon
Salmon. A fish that is enjoyed as much in France as anywhere, including *saumon fumé* (smoked salmon). *Darne de saumon* is a salmon steak.

French Sausages: A Food of Many Forms

France has a huge variety of sausages ranging from the fiery *merguez*, which has to be cooked, to *saucisse l'ail* (garlic sausage). Air-dried sausages, sometimes called *saucissons de montagne* are eaten raw, others need poaching or frying first. Use your common sense when buying. On the whole, the large sausages (*saucissons*) are pre-cooked, ready to slice and eat, the small ones (*saucisses*) will need cooking. If you object to eating horse, avoid any sausage which has the word *cheval* attached to it. Despite any dark thoughts you might have on the subject, French *charcutiers* must, by law, declare the contents of sausages made from mule, horse or donkey.

Saumon blanc
Not salmon at all, but the humble hake.

◆ Saupiquet
An ancient sharp sauce made with wine and spices, like ginger and cinnamon. Sometimes served with roast hare.

Sauté
Food, sometimes meat but usually slices of potato, cooked quickly in shallow oil or fat over high heat. The trick of success with this method is to make sure

that the pieces are all of the same size and will, therefore, be ready at the same time.

◆ Savarin
Classic light, sponge-like ring, often cooked in a decorative mould, made with yeast batter. It is covered with syrup and fruit, then drenched in rum.

◆ Savaron
A daunting-looking round cheese from Auvergne with a thick covering of mildew on the outside. Actually it has a mild taste, is semi-hard and made from cows' milk.

Scarole
Curly leaved Batavian endive. One of the slightly bitter ingredients that the sensible French include in their green salads. Delicious with dressing, it makes most lettuce seem bland and characterless.

Scorsonère, scorzonera
See SALSIFIS.

Seiche
Cuttlefish. You will occasionally find this mixed in with seafood dishes. Basically rather tough to eat, cuttlefish is beaten before cooking, then sliced and cooked like octopus, with which you may confuse it.

Sel
Salt.

Selle
Saddle, of lamb or goat.

◆◆ Selles-sur-Cher
The name of a place in the Loire et Cher district and also a fine AOC goats' milk cheese, whose rind is dusted with black powdered charcoal. It also goes under the name of *Romorantin*, and has a delicate mild flavour.

Selon grosseur
Price according to size, for example for lobster.

◆ Septmoncel, bleu de
A blue cheese from the Jura, made from cows' milk. It has a rather sharp taste and is very similar to BLEU DE GEX, made near by.

Sole
Sole. This fish is found extensively in northern France and is used for a number of classic dishes.

◆ Sole bonne femme
Sole poached in white wine with mushrooms.

◆ Sole Colbert
Sole coated in egg and breadcrumbs, then fried and served with maître d'hôtel butter.

◆◆ Sole dieppoise
Sole cooked with mussels, crayfish and white wine.

◆ Sole meunière
Sole fried with lemon and herbs.

◆◆◆ Soubise
Onion cream sauce, made with a purée of onions and rice. Usually served with meat.

◆ Soumaintrain
A strong cheese from Burgundy, made with cows' milk. It has a slightly spicy flavour, and is round and flat with a red–brown skin.

Soupe
Soup. Although soup does not appear on the menu quite as frequently as it used to, you will still find it in the country. The difference between *soupe* and *potage* is that the former tends to be on the hearty side – almost a meal in itself – whereas *potage* is usually of a less filling consistency.

◆◆ Soupe à l'ail
Garlic soup. Usually found in the Basque district, anywhere in the direction of Spain.

The onion-seller's wares

◆◆ Soupe à l'oignon
The famous French onion soup, served with grated cheese and chunky bread.

◆◆◆ Soupe au pistou
From the south, a soup with a distinct flavour of basil as well as garlic, containing vegetables and pasta (see recipe pages 97–8).

◆◆◆ Soupe de poisson
A smooth fish soup from the Mediterranean. Served with squares of toast, ROUILLE and grated cheese. It differs from the well known BOUILLABAISSE in that there are no chunks of fish or bones in it, everything having been sieved (see recipe pages 98–9).

Spécialité
Speciality.

Steack
Beef steak. The French no longer flinch if you ask it to be *bien cuit* (well done) but get their revenge in a more subtle way by serving it up almost burnt to a cinder.

Sucre
Sugar.

Suprème
Although the word sounds as though it is referring to the quality of the meat, it actually means breast of chicken, or occasionally of game bird.

T

◆◆ Tamié
A cows' milk cheese made by the Trappist monks at the monastery of Tamié, near Lake Annecy. It is smooth and round, and sometimes goes under the name of *Trappiste de Tamié*.

◆◆ Tapenade
A Provençal paste made from capers pounded with anchovies with a little olive oil and lemon. It is mushroom coloured, and looks more innocuous than it actually is. Tapenade is usually served in little pots as an appetiser, with chunks of toasted French bread.

Occasionally you will be offered it in bars.

Tapéno
Caper. These seeds of a Mediterranean shrub look and taste very like the nasturtium seeds, which are often used as a substitute.

◆ Tartare
A sharp sauce made from mayonnaise with capers, gherkins and herbs, which is usually served with fish. It is also the brand name of herb-flavoured cream cheese from Périgord.

Tartine
Slice of bread and butter, sometimes jam. The name is also used for small tart or fruit loaf.

◆ Tartine suisse
Puff pastry with vanilla cream.

Terrine
Form of potted meat or pâté. The main difference between a pâté and a terrine is that the latter is usually coarser.

Tête
Head.

Tétras
Grouse.

◆ Thiézac, bleu de
A cheese very like BLEU D'AUVERGNE which also comes from the Auvergne area. It is made from cows' milk.

Thon
Tuna fish.

Tian
Provençal word for food baked, sometimes grilled, in a shallow dish.

Tiède
Warm. *Salade tiède*, currently fashionable, is a green salad over which a warm dressing, sometimes with lardons of bacon, is poured.

◆ Tignes, bleu de
Another of the family of blue cheese from Savoie. It is small and round and made from cows' milk.

Tomme
There are literally hundreds of *tomme* cheeses, all totally different. This is because the word refers to the container in which the cheeses, usually from mountainous areas, are made.

◆ Tomme d'Annot
A cheese from the Haute-Alpes made from goats' or ewes' milk.

◆◆ Tomme de Cantal
A cheese from the Dordogne and usually made from cows' milk but sometimes from goats' milk. It is used a great deal in cooking.

◆◆ Tomme de Savoie
A larger cheese from the Savoie mountains. It is made with cows' milk and has a fairly firm texture.

◆◆ Tomme du Mont-Ventoux
A cheese from the mountain of that name which overlooks the Luberon valley in Provence. Made from ewes' milk, it is fresh and slightly salted.

Tournedos
Small beef fillet.

◆ Tournedos Rossini
Steak with truffles, *foie gras* and Madeira sauce.

◆ Tournon Saint-Pierre
A cone-shaped cheese from Poitou-Charente. It is made from cows' milk and has a strong smell, although its texture is soft.

◆◆ Touron
Nut-covered almond pastry from the South of France.

Tranche
Slice, rasher. A *tranche* can also mean a chop, so do not be surprised if it has bones.

Tripe, tripailles
Tripe, a food that is still popular in France.

◆◆ Tripe, oeufs à la
Nothing whatsoever to do with tripe but a name for chopped hard-boiled eggs with onions, from Normandy.

◆◆◆ Tripes à la mode de Caen
Tripe stewed with onions and herbs in cider and/or CALVADOS; probably the most classic tripe dish.

◆◆ Troo
The name of the cheese from the place in the Loire Valley where the late British cookery writer, Jane Grigson, lived. It is made from goats' milk and is mild and cone-shaped.

◆◆◆ Truffado
A delicious savoury dish of potatoes fried with bacon, garlic and cheese which comes from Auvergne.

◆◆◆ Truffe
Truffle. A great and very expensive delicacy in France, truffles taste rather like highly perfumed mushrooms. Known as 'black gold', they are hunted out from the roots of truffle oak trees in the Dordogne and Provence by men with specially trained dogs – originally pigs were used. Truffles are used mainly for garnishes as their price puts them out of court as the main feature of a meal. If you want to try truffles for yourself, buy a minuscule amount, set them among a bowl of eggs so that their perfume permeates the shells, then use them to make delicious truffle omelettes.

Truffe, truffé, trufflée
Garnished or stuffed with truffles. The small square of dark brown decoration in the aspic on a cold dish will almost certainly be a truffle.

Truite
Trout. *Truite arc-en-ciel* is rainbow trout. *Truite de mer* is salmon trout.

V

◆ Vachard
A strong cheese from the Massif Central made, as the name suggests, from cows' milk. It is very similar to SAINT-NECTAIRE.

◆◆ Vacherin
Meringue filled with strawberries, ice-cream and whipped cream. It is also the name given to several cheeses made from cows' milk. They are usually as soft and runny as BRIE, and come from the Jura or the Savoie mountains.

◆ Valençay
A goats' milk cheese from the Loire. It sometimes goes under the name of *pyramid*, and that is its shape.

Vapeur, au
Steamed, usually referring to potatoes.

Varié
Assorted; *hors d'oeuvres variés*, for instance.

Veau
Veal. It is used throughout France, particularly in the north. *Escalope de veau* is a flattened veal slice, which may be served in many different ways. A *paupiette de veau* is a slice of veal rolled round a filling, often pâté or ham.

◆ Veau, blanquette de
Breast of veal cooked in a white sauce.

◆◆ Venaison
Venison. Found often in country cooking, especially in hunting areas. It is usually served casseroled, often with chestnuts. It has a very rich flavour and a little goes a long way.

◆ Vendôme
The name given to a pair of cows' milk cheeses from the Loire, one a blue version.

Vermicelle
Vermicelli.

Vert(e)
Green, as in *salade verte*.

Verte, sauce
Green herb mayonnaise.

◆ Vézelay
A Burgundian cheese made from goats' milk. It comes in a conical shape and has a rather strong flavour.

Viande
Meat.

◆◆ Vichyssoise
Famous, smooth and creamy leek and potato soup. Usually served chilled but equally good piping hot in winter.

Vigneron, à la
Usually meat, served with a wine sauce of some kind, garnished with grapes.

Vinaigre
Vinegar. Plain vinegar in France is wine vinegar, less acrid than malt vinegar. It is worth taking home a bottle of French vinegar if you have space in your luggage. The French have an enormous number of flavoured vinegars, most of them wine-based (*vinaigre de vin*). The best known are tarragon vinegar (*vinaigre d'estragon*) and raspberry vinegar (*vinaigre framboise*) which is sometimes used over salads but more often as a base for a sauce with, say, liver. Both are very easy to make at home: you simply steep the flavouring in the vinegar for two or three weeks, then strain.

◆◆◆ Vinaigrette, sauce
Classic French salad dressing made with vinegar and oil. To give it a personal signature, cooks add their own extras: a spot of sugar, perhaps, some mustard or garlic (see recipe page 95).

Volaille
Poultry.

Vol-au-vent
Puff pastry case filled with meat or fish.

W

◆◆ Waldorf
Salad of apple, walnut and celeriac. An American idea which you often see served in France.

◆ Washington
Another American-inspired dish: usually chicken served American style with sweetcorn.

Williams
Type of pear. A pear is quite often referred to simply as Williams without the addition of the word *poire*.

Witloof
Chicory.

Y

Yaourt
Yoghurt. It comes in every conceivable flavouring now in the supermarkets, with full-fat and low-fat versions.

THE WINES OF FRANCE

France is undisputedly the greatest wine-producing country in the world. You will find here a vast variety of whites, reds and rosés, from the best quality vintages down to a humble *vin de pays* (local wine). The wines are basically made the same way, but how they turn out depends, to a large extent, on the choice and colour of the grape and how long they are allowed to remain in the fermenting vats. That being so, rosé wines do not keep very well, white wines have a relatively short life, and it is the heavier reds that you buy to lay down for years to come.

The largest wine-producing areas are in the centre of France – Bordeaux and Burgundy (Bourgogne), both on roughly the same parallel – while the best known must be Champagne, further north.

Wines basically fall into two categories, still or sparkling, but there is a third type that you will come across, particularly in places like Vouvray, and that is a *pétillant* – a wine with a slight natural bubble in it that just prickles on the tongue.

Apart from the extreme north, where beers and ciders hold sway, all districts of France produce a local wine of some sort. Wherever you stay, from this huge variety you are bound to find something you like to accompany a meal, whether it is one of the flowery German style Rieslings of Alsace, the light rosés from Provence that give an immediate touch of summer sun, the light-hearted Beaujolais, the heavier clarets or the important red wines from Bordeaux.

Quaffing Wines

Then there are the *ordinaires*, ordinary wines from places like Roussillon in the foothills of the Pyrenees, which are served all over France, all perfectly drinkable and cheap. If you

AC wine from the Dordogne

want to quaff wine rather than sip it appreciatively, and are therefore buying in bulk, in country areas you will find *Caves Co-operative* or the sign *Depot Vente* where *ordinaires* are served like petrol. It is a fascinating process to watch: the locals come in with plastic containers which are filled from a pump – this is the way to buy wine at a few francs a bottle. You can buy a plastic container on the spot, with or without a *robinet* (tap), to take it away in. Buying wine *en vrac* (in bulk) in this way is, of course, much cheaper but you still have a choice. If you are going for a large order, you may be surprised to be asked to sign a form and give your car registration number. This is because by French law you need a permit to carry more than three litres of wine in your vehicle: but it is only a formality, and the *Caves* do not always bother.

Appellation d'Origine
French wines are strictly controlled. The *Appellation d'Origine* system was set up, and is still governed by, the *Institut National des Appellations d'Origine* which oversees the production of wine. Four categories are used for the *appellation d'origine* classification. The highest ranking wines are the AOC wines which have an *Appellation Contrôlée*. These must come from a certain specified area, be up to a certain standard, and are strictly controlled in terms of the grapes, the growing of the vines and the production of the wine. Next down the quality list come the VDQS wines (*Vin Délimité de Qualité Supérieure*). These are superior regional wines. Then the *Vins de Pays*, good honest local wines. Finally *Vins de Table* which are the equivalent of 'plonk' but can be very good.

Recognising and Selecting Wines
All wines are named either after the grape from which they are made – Chardonnay for instance – after the name of the place where the grapes were grown, or after the place where the wine was made. It comes as a surprise, sometimes, to find that the big-name, expensive wine that you enjoy does not come from a superb château, set in rolling hectares of vines, but from a *négotiant*, a big wine shipper, like Sichel, with sober city premises. There are plenty of wines that are *mis en bouteille* (bottled) on the premises, at the vineyard of origin or the place where the wine was produced – be it a château or a humble *cave* – but many more come from grapes collected from a variety of growers and blended on warehouse premises. The word *domaine*, which is sometimes seen on the labels, also sounds like a fine country house but is probably simple a large vineyard or just a company. The fine oak casks, too, are a thing of the past in many instances, being replaced

by more hygienic high-tech tanks of fibreglass or steel. That being so, there is still a great magic about French wine, however it is made.

Finding and enjoying good wines is a fun part of any holiday. It is a shame to simply rely on the restaurant or the supermarket for bottles. It is much better to be adventurous, taste some for yourself, and then make up your own mind. Demand a tasting – not from one of the grand châteaux (you need to get an introduction from your local wine-merchant back home first) – but from the ordinary producers. The smaller the vineyard, the more likely you are to be invited in and made welcome. The word to look out for is *dégustation* (wine tasting) – you will see signs up on the road. This is not a swirl in the glass, sniff and spit session, the kind of thing that masters of wine indulge in, but a no-nonsense sampling of the wine to see, quite simply, whether you like it or not before committing yourself to a bottle. Of course, they hope you will buy but no-one will complain if you taste and then go away without purchasing anything (though, in some places, you may be charged a fractional amount per glass for the wine you consume). Even the *Caves Co-operative* have a tasting bar where you can sample their wares, and it often doubles as the local 'pub'. If you are ordering wine in a restaurant, the waiter will be delighted if you ask for a *vin de la région*, for they are bound to be proud of their own local wine.

The fruit of the vine

Cru

This term has two possible meanings when used in connection with wine. *Vin du cru* is local wine, and the term *cru* may be used to indicate that the wine is from a particular area. When used for a Bordeaux wine, the term can be taken as a mark of quality.

Cru is also used as a means of classification for wine, under the usual strict laws imposed in France. This ranges from *Premier Cru* or *Premier Grand Cru*, through *Cru Bourgeois* down to a *Cru Classé*. Any wine that comes within the *cru* classification will be of good quality, those that are *Premier Cru* or *Premier Grand Cru* are the finest and therefore the most expensive. *Cru Bourgeois* wines will also be rather expensive.

At work in the vineyard

What to Expect of the Regions

Champagne

There may be many good sparkling wines in the world but there is, quite simply, no substitute for champagne. And the reason is not just the chalky slopes on which the grapes are grown, but the immense trouble and attention to detail that goes into making this great celebratory drink. It has a freshness that no other white wine – even the splendid sparkling wines of the Loire – can quite attain. Part of the reason for this may be the use of the Chardonnay grape. Sparkling wine is made in several different ways. At the very cheapest end of the market, gas from carbonic acid is simply injected in the wine. then there is the *cuvée close* method where it is refermented in large vats. But in the *méthode champenoise* the newly made still wine is refermented the following spring in individual bottles and gradually tipped and turned, over a period, so that sediment collects at the neck from where it is ejected. The wine is then dosed with a little sugar and given the famous wired cork. All this takes a long time, and vintage champagnes are not put on sale for years. The wine is made from a mix of the white Chardonnay and the black Pinot Noir grapes. In the case of pink champagne, the skins of the black grapes are allowed to stay a little longer in the fermenting 'must' so that they colour it. Currently there is a fashion for pink champagne, which puzzles the French, as it loses some of its distinctive taste in favour of its delicate colour. If you go to Epernay there is an Avenue de Champagne, where you will find the cellars of most of the famous makers. Most of these run regular tours round their cellars, which are cut in solid chalk. Although they are rather on production line basis – in one case you are taken round in something like the ghost train on a fairground – you do get a chance to sip the product at the end.

Bordeaux

Bordeaux, in the west of France, is big in the wine business. This area produces more wine in volume than any other part of France. So it is difficult to know where to begin when talking about Bordeaux wines, for there are more fine vintages encompassed here than anywhere else in the world, especially from the Médoc to the north. There are the Saint-Emilions, the Pomerols, those from Château Lafite, Margaux and Pauillac, for instance. Bordeaux wines are so important that they are divided into *Crus*. The term takes on a special meaning for Bordeaux wines and indicates that they are of a superior quality or from a château of repute, not simply from a particular area. The red wines of Bordeaux are traditionally known in Britain and the US as clarets although the word is now used for wines from Australia and South America too. They are the fine wines to take home and leave for a year or so before you drink them. If you are likely to be impatient, choose a Pomerol, which matures relatively fast. Although Bordeaux produces three bottles of red wine to every one of white, there are a number of interesting ones in the latter category. White wines of note from this area include the sweetest wine of them all, Sauternes, which goes so well with puddings. It is made from grapes that have been left on the vine so long that they have begun to shrivel. Other white wines include the drier Entre Deux Mers which comes from an area between the two rivers, Dordogne and Garonne. Graves is an interesting wine to try: the white is relatively dry, but there is a lesser-known red Graves that is a good light luncheon drink.

Burgundy

Burgundy may not produce as large a quantity of wine as Bordeaux, but some of the best wines in the world come from its vineyards. These run in a strip along the main highway from Paris to the Mediterranean, south of Dijon. White wines such as Chablis, which makes a good partner for fish dishes, Montrachet, Meursault, Chassagne-Montrachet from Côte de Beaune, and Corton-Charlemagne are produced here, together with the elegant Pouilly-Fuissé which is extremely expensive.

On the red front, the finest burgundies come from the vineyards of the Côte d'Or which is sub-divided into the Côte de Nuits – famous for Nuits St Georges and Gevrey Chambertin – and the Côte de Beaune, the country seat of the Dukes of Burgundy, where Pommard, Volnay and Beaune itself are made. Further down comes the Mâcon district which produces both red and some very good white wines, while among the top quality but slightly cheaper reds worth trying is the full-bodied Mercurey. Sparkling wines are to be had from Rully, in the Chalon area, made properly by the *méthode champenoise*. However, big business though they may be, these wines are of less interest to the ordinary visitor to France than those of the delightful Beaujolais district around Villefranche-sur-Saône in the south, with its more informal fruity reds. The fad for Beaujolais nouveau – a rather chemical, tasteless brew – has done this district a great disservice, because there is something very special about the unpretentiousness of a real Beaujolais – and some surprises to be had. Here, among the gentle hills, are a series of villages like Brouilly, Fleurie, Juliénas, each producing its own special wine in an atmosphere which is more relaxed, less commercial. (Vaux en Beaujolais, by the way, is the origin of Clochemerle, the town in the satirical novel of the same name by Gabriel Chevallier, and there is a 'Cave de Clochemerle' in a neighbouring village, Saint-Lager, where the film of the book was made.)

Beaujolais comes in four ranks: simple Beaujolais, which is the cheapest; Beaujolais supérieur which costs a little more; then Beaujolais Villages and, finally, the wines named after the vine-yards – Chiroubles, Morgon, Chénas, Moulin-à-Vent and so on. Of all the *routes du vin* (the vineyard drives), the one through the Beaujolais region is the most rewarding. There is none of the grandeur of, say Mâcon or Beaune, because wine-making here seems to be more of a cottage industry. So make a point, if you can, of visiting these places and trying their wines. Reward the car driver by giving him or her a bottle of the best wine you taste, to drink in the evening!

The Loire

Some of the freshest, most delightful white wines of France come from this area, notably Muscadet and Gros Plant, both of which are produced around Nantes at the mouth of the river Loire. Both these wines are very dry and are ideal with seafood, found in abundance in local restaurants, or with rich chicken dishes. If you like your white wine less crisp, then try Sancerre or Pouilly-Fumé, both from the Loire valley. The red wines of the Loire, from Chinon, Saumur and Bourgueil, are lighter and softer to the taste than those of neighbouring Bordeaux, and they are a particularly good choice with lunch. Saumur also produces a sparkling wine which is fermented in the bottle by the *méthode champenoise*.

Then there are the great white wines of Vouvray to consider, made from the Chenin Blanc grape, sold sparkling, still or *pétillant*. A dry sparkling Vouvray, well chilled, can almost masquerade as champagne. If you missed out on a wine tour in the Champagne country, it is well worth touring the limestone caves of Vouvray to see how they do it. The classic rosé from the Loire is the elegant rosé d'Anjou, which cocks a snoot at its southern cousins. There is also a white Anjou wine.

Alsace

If you like the fruity flavour of German white wine, then this is the place for you. For not only are the vineyards near the German border, but the same grape varieties are grown: Gewürztraminer, Riesling, Sylvaner to name just a few.

They go perfectly with the rich rather heavy food served in the area, and even if you are not normally a fan of this strong, flowery taste, you are likely to be converted when you sample them *in situ*.

Almost all wines from Alsace and Lorraine are white but if you are visiting the area you will come across a local red which looks washed out in colour compared with one, say, from Burgundy. There is also *vin gris*, a very pale rosé, which you may be offered in local restaurants.

The wines are named by the grapes, Riesling for instance, rather than by the vineyards, which tend to remain relatively anonymous. The lightest wines are those made from the Chasselas grape. You are unlikely to find this in the bottle, but if you ask for a local wine in most cafés in Alsace, that is what you are likely to be served, usually in rather squat glasses with thick green stems.

The wines to drink before dinner, or on a summer night, are the Sylvaners. Leave the Rieslings for the main course of the meal. If you like sparkling wines, Alsace has its own local version, Crémant d'Alsace, which is fermented in the bottle like champagne. Alsace is also the place to sample a whole host of spirits based on fruits.

The South

Although few really stunning wines come from the South of France, there are some interesting ones to be found, grown in such diverse conditions as the sand of the Camargue – which produces the famous Listel branded range of wines – to the rocky soil of Corbières near Narbonne, or the stone-littered vineyards of the Rhône valley. To go with the long hot summers come a whole host of rosés which never taste quite the same, somehow, when you

Invitation in Languedoc-Roussillon

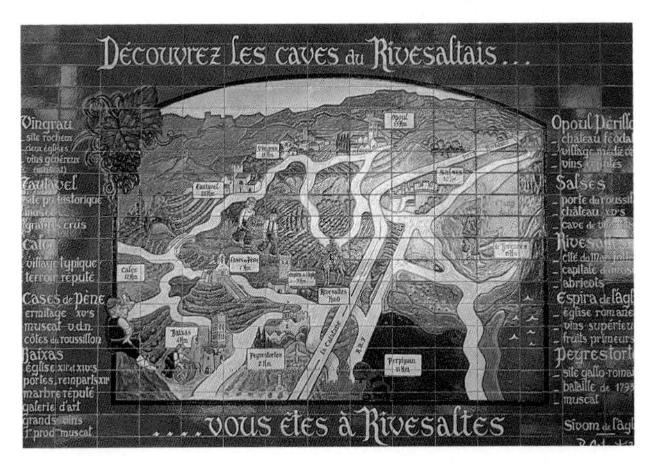

get them back home. Equally good drunk straight, iced or laced with sparkling mineral water, rosé, like *pastis* (aniseed-based drinks), is the drink of the south. The cheaper rosés are often high in alcohol, and a day supping in the sun can end in headaches.
However, a great many lighter, more elegant, wines are now being made. The most famous one is Tavel but there are a whole host of others like Côtes du Luberon and Côtes du Ventoux, called after the mountain of that name. Being so far south, production at this level tends to be of red or rosé rather than white wines. The white wine called Cassis has nothing to do with the blackcurrant liqueur, but is called after the small coastal resort of that name near Marseille.
The vineyards of the Languedoc–Roussillon area produce a large number of ordinary country wines – red, rosé and white – in large quantities. The white wines come from the area around Narbonne, near the coast, and there is a sparkling white wine from Limoux which is made the champagne way and, therefore, keeps its bubbles. Apart from Corbières, another good red wine comes from Minervois.
The great red wines of the south come from the Rhône Valley, with Châteauneuf-du-Pape as the best known one. There are many good simple Côtes du Rhône, too, some of them with AOC ratings. Provence, on the other hand, is best known for its rosés and for a very sweet, golden dessert wine called Muscat de Beaumes de Venise.

Wine List

The wines shown here are just a personal selection from the vast variety – over 700 at the last count – to be found in France. The grape varieties used in the making of the wines are shown. There is a reason for this: having found a grape variety whose taste appeals to you – the rich blackberry-like Cabernet-Sauvignon for instance, or the flowery, fruity Germanic tones of a Sylvaner or Riesling, it is on the cards that if you are choosing blind, another wine made from the same grape will suit.
If you are travelling it always pays to ask for a local wine in restaurants. Not only will you earn the proprietor's approval, but it will normally be served with great pride, and you will be told all about it.

◆◆ Alsace

Sylvaner, Riesling, and Gewürztraminer . . . most of the wines in this area are named after the grapes from which they are grown, are white and have a distinctly grapey, Germanic flavour. Wines labelled Gewürztraminer have a slightly spicier taste than the others, while the Riesling is the driest and most delicate. You will also find a light red, again called after a grape – the Pinot Noir.

◆◆ Beaujolais

Made from the Gamay grape, this jolly, red AC wine is lighter than those from Bordeaux. It can tend to be rather uninteresting, so it is worth paying a little extra for a Beaujolais Villages, one step up in quality. Better still are the named village wines like

Juliénas, Moulin-à-Vent, Fleurie or Brouilly, which is probably the best of them all. Beaujolais nouveau, the young wine that is so fashionable, should be drunk slightly chilled rather than left to develop an aroma that may well recall chemicals.

◆◆◆ **Bordeaux**
Almost undoubtedly the greatest wine-making area in France and the place where the famous names come from. Wines from this area have long been popular with the British, and Bordeaux's Atlantic position has also led to a strong US connection. Bordeaux wines, most of them red, are inclined to be heavy and rather dry. Unlike wines from Burgundy which can be drunk quite young, they should be allowed to age a little, if possible, or the taste of tannin may make your palate curl. A cheap Bordeaux wine should be treated kindly – open it at least two hours before serving it, decant it if possible. Or save up and buy a *grand cru* like St Emilion. Made mainly from the Merlot grape, it has a less harsh taste than some of the other clarets when young, and is a good buy.

◆◆◆ **Chablis**
A white AC Burgundy (the wine actually has a greenish tinge) made from the Chardonnay grape, which also produces champagne. It goes well with shellfish and hors d'oeuvres, and comes in three qualities: *grand cru, premier cru* and *petit Chablis*, which should be drunk within three years. Names to look out for include the Petit Chablis from the *négotiant* A Bichot & Co.

The vendange*: picking the grapes*

◆◆◆ **Champagne**
The world's most famous wine which must, by law, only come from the vineyards of the Champagne district around Reims. Vintage champagnes can cost an amazing amount of money, but non-vintage varieties can still be found at reasonable prices. You will be surprised to find, however, that you have to pay almost as much for it in France as in England. It is made from the Chardonnay grape, often blended with a little Pinot Noir. Pink champagne has become a popular drink recently, too.

Vineyard of the Côte du Rhône

There is nothing that tastes exactly like the real thing, but a good substitute, at a pinch, is a dry (brut) sparkling Vouvray.

◆◆◆ Château Mouton-Rothschild

One of the most famous wines in the world which, along with Château Lafite and Château Latour all come from the village of Pauillac in the Médoc. Expect to pay a great deal of money for these wines, but to drink one is an unforgettable experience – especially if someone else is footing the bill.

◆◆ Châteauneuf-du-Pape

The best-known classic AC Rhône red with a purple tinge and high alcohol content. Again this is made from a blend of up to a dozen different grapes including the strong Syrah, possibly Carignan too. The vineyard was set up for the Popes when they ruled from Avignon in the 14th century. After a disagreement with Châteauneuf du Pape, one of the popes, John XXII, set up his own vineyard near by. Look out for his label and for an interesting wine at half the price of Châteauneuf. These wines need strongly flavoured food to go with them.

◆◆ Côtes du Rhône

A robust red, with a high alcohol content – at least 12 degrees – from the Rhône valley. It is made from a mix of grapes, including almost certainly Syrah. Quality varies tremendously, but if you open the bottle and allow the wine to breathe for a couple of hours before serving it (better still, decant it), it seems to take away the rough edge. A good working red to drink with strongly flavoured dishes including pasta ones. Try Gigondas, Lirac, Cairanne or Vacqueyras.

◆ Entre Deux Mers

An old-fashioned, rather thin AC white wine from Bordeaux, currently being given a new lease of life and better quality by the wine producers. It is well worth a try.

◆ Fitou
The first time you try a young Fitou you might be forgiven for thinking it tastes like ink. However, it improves with age, and is currently a smart choice. It comes from the Corbières region of Languedoc–Roussillon, has an elegant looking label and is an AC wine.

◆ Graves
Another classic, but rather characterless AC white wine. Sometimes sweet but more usually dry, made from Sauvignon blanc and Semillon grapes, it comes from Bordeaux. There are also red Graves which are rather more interesting. The expensive and elegant Château Haut-Brion is one.

◆◆◆ Médoc
The generic name given to a range of AC wines coming from the area of that name in Bordeaux and including very expensive, great wines like Château Margaux. A wine simply labelled Médoc is usually a better choice with your meal than one called claret or any other ordinary Bordeaux. Wines labelled AC Haut-Médoc are of a slightly better quality and, therefore, more expensive.

◆◆ Mercurey
This wine from Burgundy's Côte Chalonnaise is expensive, but it has a splendid, classy flavour and does not need to be kept for a long time as it matures quicker than many others from the area. Like many Burgundy wines, it is often labelled under the name of a *négotiant*, or shipper. A reliable one to look for is Bouchard-Aîné.

◆◆ Meursault
Another classy white burgundy from the Montrachet area of Burgundy; it is drier and less heavy than the Montrachet wines and goes well with fish.

◆◆◆ Montrachet
One of several famous AC white wines, some of them *grand cru*, from the Burgundy area. Look out for Chevalier-Montrachet and Chassagne-Montrachet.

◆ Muscadet
A dry white wine from the Loire made from a grape of that name which at its best is crisp and delicious, at its worst sharp and vinegary. It goes well with all kinds of fish, particularly shellfish. Muscadet de Sèvre et Maine, an AOC wine, is a safe choice, with Muscadet des Coteaux de la Loire a close second. Muscadet *sur lie* is wine that has been bottled while it still has a slight buzz to it – in other words it is still fermenting.

◆◆ Nuits-St-George
A famous Burgundy red, a name that almost everyone knows. It comes from the Côte de Nuits, and at one time had a bad reputation for suspect wines at high prices. Now it is a strictly controlled *appellation contrôlée*, well worth drinking if slightly expensive.

◆◆ Pommard
A generic name for a group of fruity AC reds from Burgundy in the Côte de Beaune area. Individual names to look for on the label include Clos Micot and Clos des Epeneaux and the prestigious Les Rugiens.

Château d'Yquem, home of a famous premier grand cru *Sauternes*

◆◆ Pouilly-Fuissé
A golden AC wine from the Mâconnais in Burgundy, best drunk young. It goes well with white meat, fish or hors d'oeuvres.

◆◆ Pouilly-Fumé
Made from the Chenin Blanc grape, it is a slightly heavier AC white than Sancerre, its near neighbour. It cuts through rich sauces, goes well with fish and has an elegant finish.

◆◆◆ Romanée-Conti
One of the smallest and most exclusive vineyards in the world – it only covers 1.8 hectares – which produces a *grand cru* red burgundy which rates as one of the top international wines.

◆◆ Sancerre
Crisp delicious white AC wine from the Loire valley made from the Sauvignon Blanc grape. It goes well with fish, of course, but with white meats too. If you want to progress in quality from Muscadet, this is a good wine to try.

◆◆ Sauternes
A sweet white AC wine made mainly from the Semillon grape which is allowed to stay late on the vine to develop more sugar. It has unfairly gone out of fashion, but it makes a wonderful partner to puddings.

◆◆◆ Tavel
The best rosé in France (though the makers of Anjou may dispute that remark), made from the Grenache grape in vineyards in the Rhône valley. Do not drink it too cold or you will miss its elegant flavour. It goes well with fish or white meat, and makes a pleasant summer aperitif.

◆ Volnay
A light AC red from Burgundy that can be drunk very young. The vineyards are situated between Pommard and Meursault, and white wines grown in Volnay are sold as Meursault.

◆◆ Vouvray
Delicious white AC wine, well worth keeping, that comes from the vineyards of the Loire Valley. It is made from the Chenin Blanc grape, and the bottles are stored in limestone caves – worth a visit if you are in the area. Some types of Vouvray are slightly *pétillant*. Vouvray made in the *méthode champenoise* is a relatively cheap festive drink.

A–Z OF DRINKS

A

◆◆◆ Abricotine
A liqueur made from brandy and flavoured with apricots.

◆ Absinthe
Another name for wormwood, a bitter herb used to flavour vermouth. Also name of a drink now banned.

◆ Ambassadeur
Type of aperitif made with quinine, gentian, herbs, orange.

◆◆ Ameleon
A kind of cider from Normandy.

◆ Amer Picon
An aperitif containing gentian, quinine and orange – the latter probably to disguise the bitterness of the gentian.

◆ Anisette
Liqueur flavoured with aniseed.

AOC Appellation d'Origine Contrôlée
A sign that a wine complies with strict government control of origin and production method (see page 68).

◆◆◆ Armagnac
Type of brandy, often of high quality, from the Landes region.

Aperitifs
France has an enormous number of aperitifs. Most of them are strongly flavoured with herbs, some of them bitter ones like wormwood, and many of them taste like medicines. The best thing to do, if you are curious, is to order one thimbleful in a café and pass it round. One point to remember, however, if you are driving: some of them pack a hefty punch, often containing double the quantity of alcohol in wine, so take a look at the label before ordering another round.
The aniseed-based drinks, the pastis as they are called, are PERNOD and RICARD, both of which turn white and cloudy when water is added to them. Drink them with care, remember their alcohol content is roughly that of whisky, and dilute them well.
Gentian, with a slightly bitter taste, is used to flavour the vivid-yellow coloured SUZE, quinine goes into ST RAPHAEL, while AMER PICON contains the lot: gentian, quinine and orange as well. Dubonnet with its very sweet taste, seems to have gone out of fashion.

B

◆◆ Badoit
One of the cheapest mineral waters. It has a just-discernible sparkle to it, is slightly salty and comes from the Loire.

◆◆◆ Bénédictine
From Fécamp, Normandy, this was once made there by the monks of that order. It contains not one but several brandies and a mix of herbs.

Bière
Beer. French beer tends to be lightweight, like a lager, unless you are in the Alsace–Lorraine area where the German

influence is felt, or near the Belgian border. If you order a beer in a café you will be given the choice of *bouteille* (bottled) or *pression* from the pump.

Brut
Extra dry.

◆◆ Byrrh
A heavily advertised vermouth-like aperitif.

C

Café
Coffee.

◆◆◆ Calvados
Type of spirit. Made in Normandy, it has the same status as brandy but is distilled from apples not grapes. There is a tradition in the area to have a *trou Normand*, a tot of Calvados, between courses during a large meal.

Choice of Coffee
Select the coffee to suit your taste and you have the basis of the classic continental breakfast or an agreeable after-dinner digestive. Decaffeinated coffee is *faux café* or *décaféine*, *café crème* is white coffee with milk or cream, as is *café au lait*. *Café nature* and *café noir* are simple plain black coffees, while *café express* is espresso coffee. With a *café filtre*, the coffee is dripped through a filter into a jug or into the cup beneath. *Café gallois* is Irish coffee and *café glacé* is iced coffee. *Café complet* is coffee 'complete' with bread or croissants, a way of ordering breakfast. Usually white coffee is served for breakfast.

Carafe
Decanter, bottle. *Vin en carafe* (decanted wine) is usually an *ordinaire*, and the cheapest on the menu.

◆◆ Cassis, crème de
The blackcurrant spirit, often wrongly compared with blackcurrant cordial – a mistake, as you will soon find out if you down several glasses. This is an attractive, very sweet liqueur with a deep, mauve-red colour. It is usually served with white wine in a pleasant drink known as *vin blanc cassis* or *kir*. *Kir royale*, incidentally, is made with champagne, or occasionally, some other sparkling wine. Cassis is made in the Burgundy district where enormous quantities of blackcurrants are grown. *Sirop de cassis*, by the way, does not contain alcohol.

Chai
Wine cellar.

◆◆ Chartreuse
This is still made by Carthusian monks. It comes in two colours, green and the sweeter yellow type. As well as brandy it is said to contain more than 100 different herbs, and honey too.

Chope
A mug, usually for beer.

◆◆ Cidre
Cider. It is made mainly in Normandy (though some comes from Brittany) from real old-fashioned cider apples grown around the valley of the Auge. It comes in two versions, still or sparkling (*bouche*). Both

have an innocent, light refreshing taste; but they can take you unawares and you may unwittingly find yourself roaring drunk. There is also a type of perry made from pears (*poire*) which is sweeter than cider and less interesting.

◆◆◆ **Citron pressé**
Freshly squeezed lemon juice, usually served with sugar and water.

◆◆◆ **Cognac**
The best known French brandy.

◆◆ **Cointreau**
An orange-flavoured liqueur from Angers in the western Loire.

◆ **Contrexéville**
A still mineral water from the Vosges with a rather salty flavour.

◆◆ **Curaçao**
An orange-flavoured liqueur.

D

◆ **Dubonnet**
A very sweet, red vermouth-type aperitif.

E

Eau de Seltz
Soda water. PERRIER is usually substituted.

Cognac and Armagnac

Cognac The best-known French brandy distilled from relatively ordinary wine, comes from the area of that name in the Poitou–Charentes. It is sold under famous names like Martel, Remy Martin, Courvoisier, Hine and Hennessy.

Armagnac Its less-publicised rival, comes from an area in the Landes, further south. It is darker in colour and has no brand names that would be immediately recognisable to the average drinker except, perhaps, Janneau.

In both cases there are so many varieties that if you ask simply for a Cognac or an Armagnac, you will be presented with a list to choose from. However, the locals do not treat them with such reverence and often lace them with fresh grape juice and drink them as an aperitif. This drink can be bought bottled as Pineau de Charentes in Cognac and Floc de Gascogne, made in Armagnac.

Armagnac, brandy from Gascony

◆ Eau-de-vie
Basically a clear spirit sometimes made from grapes but more often distilled from fruit. In fact almost anything edible you can think of tends to be snatched off the bush or tree, distilled, then turned into a drink. Apples, plums, pears, cherries and more esoteric things, like holly berries and brambles, are all to be found in the form of a fiery spirit. A great many of these drinks seem to be made in mountainous areas like the Jura and Alsace. Look for a very good one made from pears.

Eau douce
Fresh water.

Eau minérale
Mineral water. There is a large selection of mineral waters in France, and each area tends to be partisan about its own. They can be still (*plate*) or sparkling (*gazeuse*). Their flavours range from the very bland, which just tastes like fresh spring water, to those with a salty or sharp, almost medicinal, flavour. Everyone makes claims for the efficacy of their waters – CONTREXVILLE, for instance, is supposed to be good for the kidneys – but basically, unless you have a health problem, it simply comes down to personal preference. PERRIER, with its distinctive green club-shaped bottle is the best known and is available everywhere. However, it is more expensive than many others.

Eau nature
Plain water.

Eau potable
Pure drinking water.

◆◆ Evian
A still mineral water from the town of that name on Lake Geneva. It has very little taste.

F

Fine
A type of basic, unbranded brandy. It is often drunk *à l'eau* (with water). If you ask for *une fine* in a restaurant, you may well be brought Cognac or Armagnac.

◆ Fraise des bois
An EAU DE VIE made from wild strawberries.

◆ Framboise
An EAU DE VIE made from raspberries.

G

Gazeuse
Fizzy water.

◆ Gentiane
Local liqueur from Auvergne, with a bittersweet taste.

Glaçons
Ice cubes.

◆◆ Grand Marnier
Orange-flavoured and -coloured liqueur.

◆ Grenadine
Syrup of pomegranate. Used in rum punches and other mixed drinks. Found more in the French Caribbean than in France itself.

◆ Guignolet
Cherry-flavoured spirit from the Loire. It is often thought of as a German or Austrian drink, but it is also made in the Haute Saône at Fougerolles, not far from the German border.

Liqueurs
The French have a rather old-fashioned passion for sweet liqueurs and they produce some weird and wonderful concoctions, which look like liquid sweets but can be over 50 per cent proof. The name *crème* is used for sweet liqueurs, for example CRÈME DE CASSIS (blackcurrant), *crème de banane* (banana) or *crème de cacao* (chocolate, made from cocoa beans). Most of them are less exotic and locally made; these do not travel, in that they are probably not on sale out of the area. In general people either love liqueurs or loathe them. If you like to finish your meal this way, then it is worthwhile experimenting with some new ones. (See under individual entries in this A–Z list.)

K

◆◆◆ **Kirsch**
Spirit distilled from cherries. It is probably the best known EAU-DE-VIE type spirit.

M

Marc
Local brandy. Some marcs are quite evil in their effect if you imbibe too much. The reputable ones like *marc de Bourgogne*, made from the last pressings of Burgundy grapes, and *marc de Champagne* are perfectly safe; but you may be offered, in a spirit of friendship, a glass of 'home brew', distilled from the last of the grape skins and pips; this should be sipped with caution.

◆ **Marie Brizard**
A well-publicised brand of liqueur, from a company which produces different kinds, ranging from an aniseed-flavoured drink, through to apricot.

◆ **Myrtilles, crème de**
A liqueur flavoured with bilberries.

O

◆ **Orangina**
Brand of soft, fizzy orange drink.

P

◆◆◆ **Pernod**
Aniseed-based aperitif (pastis).

Perrier
Mineral water used, because of its sparkle, instead of soda with drinks. It comes from the area around Nîmes. It has almost no flavour.

◆ **Pschhht**
A kind of lemonade, popular with children.

R

◆ **Ricard**
Aniseed-based aperitif (pastis).

S

◆◆◆ St Raphael
Aperitif containing quinine.
Sec
Dry; neat – for example *whisky sec* is neat whisky.
Supérieur
A name found on some Bordeaux bottles like Graves, for instance. This does not mean that the wine is superior, but that it contains 1 per cent more alcohol than the official minimum.
◆ Suze
Yellow-coloured aperitif containing gentian.

T

◆◆◆ Tisane
A herbal infusion. The French drink as many, probably more, tisanes than conventional teas, believing they have a medicinal value. The most popular is probably *tilleul*, lime-flower tea, which is soothing and refreshing. The famous cup of tea with the *madeleine*, which Marcel was drinking at the start of Proust's *A La Recherche du Temps Perdu*, was a *tilleul*.

V

◆ Verveine
Sweet liqueur with bitter undertones, from the Auvergne region.
◆◆ Vichy
A sparkling water which comes from around the town of that name.
Vin
Wine.
Vin blanc
White wine.
Vin bourru
New wine.
Vin chaud
Mulled wine.
Vin doux
Sweet wine.
Vin du cru or **du pays**
Local wine, or wine from a particular area.
Vin en carafe
Decanted into a container.
Vin en pichet
In a jug – usually a small one.
Vin gris
Pale pink wine – Listel make one.
Vin jaune
Yellow wine. Sherry-like dry wine, aged in the barrel for at least six years.
Vin mousseux
Sparkling wine, but not made in the *méthode champenoise*.
Vin muscat
Sweet dessert wine from Muscat grapes.
Vin ordinaire
Ordinary wine.
Vin rosé
Pink wine.
Vin rouge
Red wine.
Vin sec
Dry wine.
◆◆ Vittel
A still mineral water from the Nancy area with a rather earthy flavour.
◆ Volvic
A still mineral water from Auvergne, with no discernible flavour. It is filtered through volcanic rock.

SHOPPING

In this and later chapters, words and phrases are included to help you deal with everyday situations. Phonetic pronunciation guides are given, but for more information on pronouncing French see **Language** page 125.

There is a huge diversity of shopping in France. There are, on the one hand, some of the largest supermarkets outside the US and, at the other end of the scale, tiny delightful *marchés* (markets), with a stall or two set up under the trees to sell local produce.
However, it would be a shame to go on holiday and take refuge in supermarkets and markets alone when France has so many superb specialist shops. The sensible way to shop is to buy boring items like toilet paper and washing powder at the supermarket, then use the specialist shops for fun items.

Where to Shop

Alimentation Générale

Alimentation Générale is the sign that you will see over a shop that sells dairy goods, groceries, all sorts of things.

Groceries

bacon lard maigre *laR mehgR*
bread pain *paN*
butter beurre *beuR*
cheese fromage *fRomazh*
coffee, instant café enpoudre (Nescafé) *kafay ahN-poodR (neskafay)*
eggs oeufs *euh*
flour (wheat) farine de froment *faReen deu fRomahN*
ham jambon *zhahNbawN*
jam confiture *kawNfeetewR*

Useful phrases for shopping

I would like . . . j'aimerais . . . *zhemReh . . .*
do you have . . . ? avez-vous . . .? *avay voo . . .?*
some (a little) . . . du/de la/des . . . *dew/deu la/deh* . . . un peu de . . . *uN peu deu . . .*
a packet of . . . un paquet de . . . *uN pakeh deu . . .*
a slice of meat une tranche de viande *ewn tRahNsh deu vyahNd*
bigger, smaller plus grand/plus petit *plew gRahN, plew peutee*
can I help myself? je peux me servir? *zheu peuh meu seRveeR?*
don't touch! ne touchez-pas! *neu tooshay pa!*
anything else? et après? *eh apReh?*
that's it (no more) c'est tout *seh too*
how much is it? c'est combien? *seh kawNbyaN?*
go to the cash desk (till) passez à la caisse *passay a la kehss*

A specialist 'snail shop'

margarine margarine *maRgaReen*
marmalade confiture d'orange *kawNFeetewR doRahNzh*
milk lait *leh*
mineral water eau minérale *oh meeneRal*
mustard moutarde *mootaRd*
olive oil huile d'olive *weel doleev*
pasta pâtes *paht*
pepper (white, black) poivre (blanc, noir) *pwavR (blahN, nwaR)*
salt sel fin, sel de table *sel faN, sel deu tahbl*
sugar sucre *sewkR*
tea thé *teh*
vinegar vinaigre *veenehgR*

Boucherie

The *boucherie* is the butcher's shop and sells all kinds of meat, including poultry, except pork.
Cuts of meat in France are different from those in butchers' shops elsewhere, and the meat is usually cut specially for each customer. You will never see mince, for instance, out on display; instead a choice piece of beef will be specially put through the mincer for you. Meat, particularly lamb, is expensive, but of a high quality with no wastage, so you need not buy too much. Some butchers sell cooked food, including ready roasted chickens and items of charcuterie – the smaller the town or village, the wider the range. A *boucherie chevaline* sells horse meat – there is usually a horse's head 'pub' sign above the door.

Meat and poultry

beef boeuf *beuf*
chicken poulet *pooleh*
chop côtelette de . . . *kohtlett deu*
horse meat viande de cheval *vyahNd deu shval*
kidneys rognons *RonyawN*
leg of lamb gigot (d'agneau) *zheegoh (danyoh)*
liver foie *fwa*
loin of meat échine, épinée *esheen, epeenay*
minced meat la viande hachée *vyahN dashay*
mutton mouton *mootawN*
rabbit lapin *lapaN*
turkey dinde *daNd*
veal veau *voh*
venison venaison *veunezawN*

Boulangerie

The *boulangerie*, the baker's, is the most important shop in any village. There is one open every day of the week because, by French law, every village over a certain size must have a baker or a supplier of bread. And the bread is baked twice a day to ensure that it is absolutely fresh. The *boulangerie* also sells those other staple items of the French breakfast: classic crescent shaped CROISSANTS, PAINS AU CHOCOLAT, BRIOCHES and other kinds of buns. The *boulangerie* in a small village will also sell gâteaux, fruit tarts and, often, quiches and pizzas.

Casino

In small towns and larger villages, you may find shops called *Casino*. These are individually owned but members of an association or a chain. They are almost always set out on supermarket lines and are a practical place to shop for anyone whose French is non-existent or rather rusty. It is so much easier to help yourself to things rather than look up the

Bread, fresh and various

Bread – Fresh Every Day

The familiar French loaf is bought fresh every day quite simply because it becomes stale very quickly. The light texture of the bread, made from a soft flour, and its long, thin shape contribute to this. In French households, bread left over at the end of the day is likely to be placed in the bottom of the soup tureen or dunked in coffee next day.

The thinnest loaf, known as *ficelle*, is also shorter than the long, comparatively plump *baguette*. *Un baton, un pain* or *une gresson* are also names you are likely to encounter for similar, long loaves, and the thickest are *Parisien* or *gros pain*. *Petit pain* are the short versions (large rolls) and *pain épi* is a useful loaf for picnics, as it is a long stick made corn-ear style. The crunchy points of dough on *pain épi* may be broken away easily, like a series of linked bread rolls.

Wholemeal and brown bread, more plentiful now, is known variously as *pain de son, pain de siègle, pain bis, pain complet* or *pain entier*. *Pain noir* is also a term for wholemeal bread.

Soft-crusted bread, of the type often sliced for sandwiches, is known as *pain de mie*. Oval, soft-crumbed crusty loaves are *Viennois* and rings of bread (of the same type as *baguettes*) are *couronnes*.

Round, slightly flattened loaves, *pain campagne*, are not as light as sticks and they stay fresh longer.

You will also find delicious breads with nuts or olives in them, or with cheese on top. Then there are the familiar rich breads – CROISSANTS, BRIOCHES and PAIN AU CHOCOLAT (croissant-like dough made into buns with a piece of chocolate in the middle).

words for items. You will find that the proprietor will be chatty and friendly, especially when she gets to know you. Many *Casinos* have fruit and vegetables as well as grocery items and drinks.

Fruit and vegetables

apples pommes *pomm*
aubergines aubergines *ohbeRzheen*
bananas bananes *banan*
broad beans fèves *fehv*
cabbage chou *shoo*
carrots carottes *kaRott*
celery céleri *seleRee*
cherries cerises *seuReez*
chilli piment *peemahN*
courgettes courgettes *kooRzhett*
cucumber concombre *kawNkawNbR*
dates dattes *datt*
garlic l'ail *lahy*
grapefruit pamplemouse *pahNpleumooss*
grapes raisins *RezaN*
green beans haricots verts *aReekoh vaiR*
lemon citron *seetRawN*
lettuce (cos, round) laitue (romaine, beurrée) *letew (Romehn, beuRRay)*
lime limon *leemawN*
melon melon *meulawN*
mushrooms champignons *shahNpeenyawN*
onions oignons *wanyawN*
oranges oranges *oRahNzh*
peaches pêches *pehsh*
pears poires *pwahR*
peas petits pois *peutee pwa*
peppers poivrons *pwavRawN*
pineapple ananas *ananass*
plums prunes *pRewn*
potatoes pommes de terre *pom deu taiR*
strawberries fraises *fRehz*
tomatoes tomates *tomat*
vegetables légumes *legewm*

Charcuterie

The *charcuterie*, once simply a pork butcher, now tends to sell all sorts of delicatessen items, and this is the place to plunder for a picnic. Essentially, it is a cooked meat shop, although it sells pork ready for cooking as well. Here you will find PÂTÉS, TERRINES and SAUCISSES, from the air dried variety to those that need cooking. Look out for items like RILLONS, RILLETTES and pigs' ears in jelly. There will be black and white puddings (BOUDIN BLANC and NOIR), ANDOUILLETTES and the spicy hot MERGUEZ sausages as well as frankfurters, also hams and GALANTINES. There will be salad items like CELERI RAVÉ and *champignons à la grecque*, probably small quiches and pizzas. The *charcuterie* will often sell made-up dishes too or ready-cooked meals to take away – or look for these in the *traiteur* (take-away food shop). These foods usually include dishes like COUSCOUS, CHOUCROUTE, ready-roasted chickens and at least one *plat du jour* – a DAUBE, for instance. If you are buying ham, avoid *jambon de Paris* or *jambon York*, both of which tend to be tasteless; look for local hams instead. You may even find *jambon de marcassin*, which is an elegant ham made from smoked wild boar.

Charcuterie

frankfurter sausage saucisse de Francfort *soseess deu fRahNkfoR*
ham (raw, smoked) jambon (cru, fumé) *zhahNbawN kRew, fewmay*
pork porc *poR*
sausages saucisses *soseess*

Confiserie
The *confiserie* is the sweet shop, selling quality hand-made chocolates and bon-bons, nougat and crystallised fruit. France does not have a preponderance of ready-wrapped sweets. Sometimes the *confiserie* forms part of a tea-room or a *pâtisserie*. The best buy from here is undoubtedly chocolate – at a price though, with truffles topping the bill. At Easter time the confiserie shops are full of chocolate rabbits, chickens and nests of eggs. If you buy one of these, it will be elaborately gift-wrapped for you.

Epicerie
The *épicerie* is the grocer's shop, often also called *Alimentation Générale*. Except in very small villages, it is run on supermarket lines but with a counter for items like cheese and unpackaged meats.

Fromagerie
The *fromagerie* is a specialist cheese shop, usually only found in larger towns. There are more than 300 French cheeses to choose from, of which some are listed in the **A–Z of French Food**. You are never expected to buy your cheese in a *fromagerie* without tasting it first, that would be unheard of. Two types of cheese you might like to try are *fromage fort*, a fermented cheese usually flavoured with herbs, and *fromage frais*, which you will find in all shops and supermarkets. The latter is a yoghurt-like fresh 'cheese' with a bland taste. It is soft and used instead of cream with fruit.

Seasonal produce in the market

Marché
The street markets are part of the French way of life, and in every self-respecting town, one day of the week is market day – frequently Saturday. Enquire at the local *Syndicat d'Initiative* (tourist office). Apart from that, even the smallest village will have a few stalls set out, including, perhaps, a visitation from the *charcuterie* or *poissonnerie* van and a cheese seller on one special day a week. Stalls selling olives are fascinating too, with more than a dozen different types on offer – including delicious tiny ones. Local housewives also set up pavement stalls to sell their own produce, usually honey or jam – expensive but excellent. Look out for unusual conserves like

lemon and ginger. Travelling organic vegetable vans which tour the villages are now also becoming part of the scene. Markets are the best places to buy fresh flowers, fruit and vegetables in season. There will almost certainly be kitchen utensils and gadgets, crockery and cutlery. So this is the place to buy the corkscrew, the knife and any picknicking item that you forgot to pack for the holiday. Markets are a good place for children, too, as there is plenty to do and see – often a hurdy-gurdy man or a puppeteer to entertain them, or even a roundabout.

Even if your French is not all that it should be, you can get by at the market by mime – pointing, prodding and smiling. It is quite in order to ask to taste (*goûter*) a sliver of cheese, pâté or sausage, just as it is to pick out the particular fruit or vegetables that you want from a market stall. When buying things like pâté, it is better to ask for *une tranche* (a slice) rather than so many grammes, or say you are buying for 'x' number of *personnes* and leave it to the good sense of the stall holder. When it comes to fruit and vegetables, more and more market stalls and shops now provide plastic baskets or bags on display at the front. You simply help yourself, the assistant weighs it up and tells you how much it costs.

Pâtisserie

The *pâtisserie* sells cakes both large and small and, above all, impressive looking tarts and flans that are bought for the sweet course in a French home as a matter of course. There will be biscuits too. Look out for *babas* (BABA AU RHUM) and SAVARINS drowned in liqueurs, as well as MADELEINES, meringues and gâteaux like SAINT-HONORÉ and PITHIVIERS. The *pâtissière* is also very often an ice-cream maker, and you can also buy some splendid sorbets, particularly fruit-flavoured ones, at a *pâtisserie*.

Poissonnerie

The *poissonnier*, the fishmonger, very often operates from a stall or a van, rather than

Concarneau fish market, Brittany

from a shop. There is, as you would expect, an enormous range of fish to be had in France, even far inland. It is here that you will find a tray heaped with all kinds of tiny fish labelled SOUPE DE POISSON. A kilo of these will make mouthwatering soup in no time at all (see recipe pages 98–9). Look out for plump fresh sardines to grill out of doors and steaks of fresh tuna (*thon*) which are filling enough to take the place of a hearty meat meal. Try your hand with swordfish (ESPADON), octopus (POULPE) or mussels (MOULES). You will also find salted cod (MORUE) on sale, which needs soaking for 24 hours in many changes of water before use. It is used in a classic Provençal dish AIOLI GARNI, something of an acquired taste, which combines salted cod, vegetables and a garnish of snails. It used to be eaten on Fridays but is now on the menu all through the week.

Poissonnerie
anchovies anchois *ahNshwa*
bass bar *baR*
bream brème *bRehm*
carp carpe *kaRp*
clams palourdes *palooRd*
cod morue *moRew*
crab crabe *kRab*
eel anguille *ahNgweey*
fish poisson *pwassawN*
herring (smoked, salt) hereng (fumé, salé) *aRaN (fewmay, salay)*
kipper hereng saur *aRaN sohR*
lobster homard *omaR*
mackerel marquereau *makRoh*
monkfish lotte *lott*
mullet (grey, red) mulet (gris, rouge) *mewlay (gRee, Roozh)*
mussels moules *mool*
octopus poulpe *poolp*
oysters huîtres *weetR*
perch perche *peRsh*
pike brochet *bRosheh*
prawns crevettes roses *kReuvett Rohz*
salmon saumon *sohmawN*
scampi langoustines *lahNgoosteen*
shellfish crustacés *kRewstassay*
squid calmar *kalmaR*
trout truite *tRweet*
tuna thon *tawN*
whitebait blanchailles *blahNshahy*

Supermarkets
The supermarkets are mainly out of town, vast drive-in complexes where you can eat, park the children in a crèche, have your hair done, buy furniture, sports gear and, of course, food. Items tend to come in giant-size packs, and it is certainly the cheapest way to stock up with basic goods if you are catering for yourself. Names to look out for (they usually advertise themselves with huge hoardings on the highways) are *Mammouth*, *Euromarché*, *Carrefour* (one of the largest and most widespread) and *Leclerc*, which is usually cheaper than the others. Closed on Sundays, they usually stay open late in the evening, up to 21.00 or 22.00 hrs. In the south, their opening hours tend to change with the seasons, shutting for a siesta at midday in summer.
Supermarkets are useful if it is raining, when the idea of wandering round the *marché* does not appeal. You also have time to price items at your leisure and to read the labels on the products. When you get to the check-out, the cashier will

sing out the total – difficult to hear and understand quickly. So keep an eye on the till where the figures will be displayed. More and more supermarkets are now taking credit cards, which makes the business of paying much easier. Otherwise do not be afraid to spread out the small change in your hand and let the cashier help herself to the bits and pieces.

Traiteur

The *traiteur* is the housewife's friend, the take-away food shop, where you can buy ready-prepared, often ready-cooked foods, including quite elaborate dishes. This is a good way to try the local specialities of the region if you are in self-catering accommodation. Then, if you like what you taste, you can look up the recipe, and try it at home.

Other Food Shops

There are a few other shops you may encounter, such as a *volailler*, the poulterer; *crémerie*, selling dairy products and – though less and less as time goes by – a *triperie*, selling tripe with a range of sauces. Instead of the latter you may find a specialist shop selling pasta. Health food shops are now on the increase (see **Special Diets**, page 121).

Non-Food Shops

Other, non-food, shops you may need are the *pharmacie*, the chemist, which does not sell cosmetic items or soaps, but offers only medicines. Toiletry items are more likely to be found at the *droguerie*, a type of hardware store.

If you are in need of a dry cleaning service, look out for the sign *nettoyage a sec*. *Une blanchisserie* is a laundry. *Un tabac*, the tobacconist, with its distinctive red cigar-shaped sign over the door, sells stamps as well as cigarettes, cigars and possibly postcards too. A *maison de la presse* sells magazines, while a *librairie* is a bookshop, not a library – that is a *bibliothèque*. The weird-looking word *quincaillerie*, by the way, denotes a hardware shop.

When to Shop

Shopping hours vary according to what part of France you are in. Basically most shops open around 08.30 hrs, then close at noon until about 14.30 hrs or as late as 15.30–16.00 hrs during the summer in the south, when they will stay open until 18.30–19.00 hrs. Some supermarkets stay open at lunch time – a good time to shop as, because the French take their main meal of the day at lunchtime, they are almost always half empty. Most shops, and all banks, are closed on Monday. Banks also have different opening times on a Saturday and are closed on national holidays.

Going Shopping

What time do the shops open? Les magasins s'ouvrent à quelle heure? *leh magazaN soovR a kel euR?*
Are they open on Sundays? Ils sont ouverts le dimanche? *eel sawN toovaiR leu deemahNsh?*
Is there a supermarket near? Y a-t-il un supermarché près d'ici? *ee ateel uN sewpeRmaRshay pReh deesee?*

I want to buy . . . Je veux acheter *. . . zheu veuh ashtay . . .*
What time do the shops close? Les magasins se ferment à quelle heur? *leh magazaN seu feRm ta kel euR?*

What to Bring Home
There are some foods that, alas, simply do not travel well. What looks so good on a market stall may be less appealing when you get it home. Bread, of course, is a case in point: that baguette that was so crisp and fresh just before you boarded the ferry may be hard as a board by the time you go to slice it next morning. However, some breads are well worth bringing back – brown breads containing nuts, olives, onions or with toasted cheese dribbled over the top, for instance. These keep fresh for several days and will freeze well.
Cheese is difficult to transport if you buy it in the south and are coming back by car, when you may be almost overcome by its pungent smell – or it may start 'walking' as it warms up. However, an insulated picnic bag can solve that particular difficulty.
Some canned items are well worth stowing in the boot of the car. Canned petits pois with baby onions are delicious, so is canned CASSOULET. Chestnut purée and whole chestnuts in cans are a fraction of the price you would pay at home in France, as are coffee beans. Dried beans, like flageolets, are cheap and good. At one time COUSCOUS was a bring-back-home item but now you can buy the semolina grains in most

Nut oil from the Dordogne

good supermarkets. You may not, however, be able to buy the cans or tubes of HARISSA, the hot pimento paste that goes with COUSCOUS, so this is a good item to bring back. Canned pâtés do not taste particularly good but those preserved in jars last a long time and make a good buy, as do other favourite items of charcuterie which are available sealed in jars.
Any good delicatessen stocks French sausages but if you want to take home a favourite *saucisse d'ail*, for instance, it should keep for a while in the refrigerator.
Unusual *confitures* (jams) made from esoteric fruits like greengages, bilberries or mulberries are worth bringing

Tasty reminders of Brittany

back. And if you keep your eyes open at street markets, you may find home-made jams – lemon and ginger, for instance, or lime. Olives, of course, are a good buy if you like them, and so is olive oil and walnut oil.

A garlic plait will last you a long time, but the cloves do tend to dry out after a while, and they can go mouldy in damp conditions, so make it a small one.

Herbs are a fragrant reminder of your holiday. By all means buy a bunch or two to decorate the kitchen, but it is best to buy *herbes de Provence* in airtight jars or pack them that way before transporting them. Do not forget to store them out of direct sunlight when you get them home.

Canned and bottled sauces like AÏOLI, ROUILLE, sauce Nantua, Béarnaise and Hollandaise are worth bringing home. So is canned SOUPE DE POISSON – avoid the dried versions which can be disappointing. You will also find certain soups sold chilled and sealed in soft plastic bags. These are more authentic than the canned versions and worth buying if you plan to consume them immediately after a speedy return. Check the directions on the pack before you buy to avoid any risk of over-long storage and possible food poisoning. See also **Transporting Food** on page 123.

French chocolates can be delicious, but they tend to melt on long hot journeys.

On the kitchenware front, everyone knows by now that the famous le Creuset range of cast-iron ware can be bought much more cheaply in France. It is also a good idea to buy Mouli graters if you like them. Many small electrical items – tiny machines to chop herbs, coffee grinders, *sauciers* (for making sauces) – and other kitchen gadgets can often be bought more cheaply in French supermarkets than at home.

Look for good, cheap knives. Be sure to check, first, on electric appliances that the voltage is correct, for most electrical appliances on sale in France are available in 120 or 210 volts and are not suitable for a 240 volts supply. Remember too that if you have a problem with an expensive piece of equipment, returning it to the store in France will not be easy.

Cutlery and crockery too can be found cheaply in bright designs, and they are safe buys so long as you can pack them well.

RECIPES

The recipes below vary in difficulty. Those with one star (*) are simple to prepare, while those with two stars (**) are more complex and time consuming.

*Sauce vinaigrette**

Oil and Vinegar Dressing

Makes 170ml/6fl oz

Everyone eventually evolves their own recipe for making vinaigrette. But here is the classic version of the famous salad dressing. You can vary it by adding crushed garlic, a little chopped herb such as chive, a touch of mustard, pounded hard-boiled egg yolk, even sugar. The choice of oil can alter the flavour too – walnut oil, or olive oil, in particular. It is preferable to use wine vinegar, or you can substitute lemon juice. You can, of course, vary the amounts given as long as you keep to the same ratio: 3 parts oil to 1 part vinegar.

½ teaspoon salt
2 tablespoons vinegar
6 tablespoons oil
freshly ground black pepper

Put the salt into a small bowl, add the vinegar and mix well until the salt has dissolved. Add the oil gradually, beating as you go, until the mixture becomes a cloudy, slightly thick emulsion. Season to taste with black pepper. Pour over a salad just before serving.

Vinaigrette keeps well in a small bottle in the refrigerator. Shake it well before use as the oil and vinegar will tend to separate out.

*Aïoli***

Garlic Mayonnaise

Serves 4–6

This garlic-flavoured mayonnaise from the south is served in many ways, with CRUDITÉS, SOUPE DE POISSON, salads, cold meats and fish. You can also eat it with artichokes, hard-boiled eggs or chick-peas. The secret of success in making this mixture is to ensure that all the ingredients are at room temperature. Although olive oil is the classic choice for this sauce, you could use something more bland like arach (peanut or groundnut oil), if you wish. If you do not have a lemon, slightly less vinegar can be substituted for the lemon juice.

6 cloves garlic, skinned
salt and freshly ground black pepper
2 egg yolks
300ml/½ pint olive oil
2 teaspoons lemon juice

Crush the garlic with a pestle and mortar or garlic crusher, then mix it with a little salt and pepper. Whisk in the egg yolks one by one. Then add the oil drop by drop, speeding up the process when half the oil has been used.
Finally whisk in the lemon juice. If the mixture should curdle, beat an egg yolk in a separate

bowl. Gradually beat in the curdled mixture, a teaspoonful at a time at first, then a little quicker as the mixture becomes smooth and thick. With care, the *aïoli* will be rescued. If the mixture seems too stiff, add 2 teaspoons warm water.

*Anchoïade***

Anchovy Paste

Serves 4

This is very much a southern dish which is also very popular in Corsica. If you like the salty, fishy taste of anchovies, then this makes a perfect starter or snack. It is best to buy these tiny fish in oil in 50g/2oz cans. If you buy anchovies loose in brine, they will need their skins scraped and their backbones removed, then soaking in a mix of water and milk to take out some of the salt. The paste may also be served as a dip, with CRUDITÉS.

2 (50g/2oz) cans anchovies in oil
1 tablespoon olive oil
a little vinegar
stale French bread, to serve

Pound the anchovies with a pestle and mortar (a blender makes the mixture too smooth), adding the olive oil, drop by drop as though making mayonnaise, working it in well. Finish the paste by adding a little vinegar to taste.
Cut the bread into thick chunks and toast it under the grill on one side. Turn the bread chunks over, spread the anchovy paste on the soft sides and return them to the grill. Turn the heat down to warm the toast through.

*Salade de tomates**

Tomato Salad

Serves 4–6

A cheap, quickly made starter which also makes a delicious lunch dish, accompanied by chunks of French bread. Do not dismiss this simple salad as unadventurous – when deep-coloured ripe tomatoes are used the flavour is markedly different from anything that can be achieved back home. Try to obtain the large mild and sweet onions, if you can. This is a dish that improves with age – after a couple of days, the tomatoes and onions absorb the flavour of the dressing. You can also add to it by topping up from time to time with fresh slices of tomato. Add a crushed clove of garlic, if liked, or a sprinkling of fresh basil.

1 large onion, skinned
500g/1lb tomatoes
350ml/12fl oz sauce vinaigrette
(see page 95)

Chop or slice the onion, wash and slice the tomatoes. Put them in alternate layers in a bowl or shallow dish, then pour over the vinaigrette. Leave to marinate for at least 30 minutes before serving, turning them over from time to time to make sure that they absorb the dressing. Have chunks of fresh bread to mop up the juices.

Petit chèvre chaud, *cheesy starter*

*Petit chèvre chaud**

Goats' Milk Cheese Starter

Serves 4

This fashionable starter is made with goats' milk cheese but you could substitute another soft cheese such as Camembert. Two portions per person make a good lunch.

1 cylindrical goats' milk cheese, such as BANON
2 tablespoons chopped fresh herbs, such as thyme, marjoram or chives
250ml/8fl oz sauce vinaigrette (see page 95)
2 tablespoons chopped walnuts (optional)
mixed green salad

Slice the cheese into four thick chunks, place on a baking tray and sprinkle with herbs. Put the cheese under a hot grill to toast (or in a hot oven if you are without a grill). Set on one side to keep warm while you heat the vinaigrette just to blood temperature. Sprinkle the walnuts over the salad and serve it on four plates. Spoon a little warm vinaigrette over, then top with the cheese.

*Soupe au pistou***

Hearty Vegetable Soup with Basil Paste

Serves 4

A famous vegetable soup from Nice. PISTOU is a corruption of the Italian word pesto, *a paste made with basil, which gives the soup its special flavour. Traditionally you should add pine nuts (*pignons*), Italian style, to the basil paste. Pine nuts can be found all over France and can now be bought easily in health food shops at home.*

2 tablespoons oil
1 onion, skinned and sliced
2 tomatoes, skinned and chopped
salt and freshly ground black pepper
250g/8oz fresh haricot beans
250g/8oz green beans, cut into short lengths
1 courgette, chopped
2 large sticks of celery, chopped
2 potatoes, peeled and chopped
50g/2oz vermicelli

For the pistou:
8 sprigs of fresh basil
2 cloves garlic, skinned
½ tablespoon pine nuts
2 tablespoons olive oil
1 tablespoon grated Parmesan cheese

Ingredients for soupe au pistou

Heat the oil in a large pan, add the onion and cook gently until golden in colour – about 20 minutes or more. Stir in the chopped tomatoes, season, then add about 750ml/1¼ pints water and bring to the boil. Add the haricot beans and simmer for 10 minutes, then put in the green beans, courgette, celery and potatoes. Leave to simmer for 30 minutes.
Meanwhile make the pistou: pound the basil leaves together with the garlic and pine nuts in a pestle and mortar or blender. Add the oil, drop by drop, then mix in the grated Parmesan.
When the soup is ready, add the vermicelli and bring it back to the boil. Take a cupful of soup mixture, stir in the pistou sauce, then return it to the pan. Simmer for 5 minutes and serve.

*Soupe de poisson***

Fish Soup

Serves 6

It is the saffron that gives this soup its traditional yellow–red colour. If you are unable to find it, then turmeric (curcuma) *will do. You will find the fish on sale in markets all over the south, simply known as* soupe de poisson. *The mix must include the* rascasse, *a small ugly red fish. To prepare this soup properly, you need a Mouli sieve which will filter out the bones. This soup is traditionally served either with* AÏOLI *or* ROUILLE, *slices of toasted French bread and grated cheese.*

1kg/2lb mixed small fish
3–4 tablespoons olive oil
2 cloves garlic, skinned and crushed
2 onions, skinned and sliced
2 Marmande-type or beef tomatoes, roughly chopped, plus 2 large tomatoes, chopped
a large piece of fennel, sliced
sprig of parsley
¼ teaspoon saffron strands
1 bay leaf
300ml/½ pint dry white wine
125g/5oz vermicelli, broken into short lengths
salt and freshly ground black pepper
slices of toasted French bread
75g/3oz grated Parmesan cheese

For the rouille:
2 slices French bread
2 cloves garlic
¼ teaspoon salt
2 canned red peppers
olive oil

Wash and pick over the fish. Scale the larger pieces and gut them if necessary but leave heads and tails on the small fish. Heat the oil in a large pan and fry the garlic and onion for a few moments. Stir in the tomatoes, fennel, parsley, then the fish, together with a few strands of saffron and the bay leaf. Meanwhile pound the remaining saffron to a powder. Stir the fish mixture well and cook over a medium heat for 5 minutes gently crushing the saffron strands as the mixture cooks. Add 2 litres/3½ pints water, the wine and powdered saffron. Bring to the boil and simmer, uncovered, for 20 minutes, skimming off any froth. Take out the bay leaf, then pass the mixture through a Mouli sieve (you can use a blender but the effect is not quite the same). Bring the soup back to the boil, add the vermicelli, adjust the seasoning, and cook for a further 15 minutes.
To make the rouille, soak the bread in a little water for 5 minutes. Then squeeze it dry until it is like a wrung-out flannel. Crush the garlic with the salt, peppers and bread in a pestle and mortar. Add oil gradually until you have a thick paste. Serve the soup piping hot with bowls of grated Parmesan and rouille. Traditionally you spread toasted slices of French bread with the rouille, then float them on the top, either sprinkling cheese over the soup itself or over the toast.

*Salade niçoise**

Vegetable Salad with Olives and Anchovies

Serves 4

Everyone has a favourite version of salade niçoise. According to what you put in it, this salad can be a filling lunch dish or just an attractive starter. But common to every version are two things – olives and anchovies. This version would make a fairly filling lunch. If you want it to be even more substantial, add some cooked young artichoke hearts and chunks of canned tuna. Though not a traditional ingredient, lettuce – preferably the crisp type – can be added.

- 1 clove garlic, skinned and cut in half
- 2 eggs
- 500g/1lb tomatoes, skinned and quartered
- ½ cucumber
- 1 red or green pepper, seeded and sliced
- handful of cooked French beans, cut into short lengths
- 1 medium onion, skinned and sliced
- salt and freshly ground black pepper
- 1 (50g/2oz) can anchovies
- 12 black olives, stoned
- 4 tablespoons sauce vinaigrette, preferably made with tarragon vinegar (see page 95)
- 1 tablespoon chopped fresh parsley

Rub the inside of a wooden salad bowl with the cut clove of garlic. Hard-boil the eggs. Plunge them in cold water to stop the yolks from blackening, then shell them and set aside to cool. Skin the cucumber using a potato peeler or sharp knife, then chop it by slicing down the length into four 'planks' and cutting across. Put the prepared vegetables in the salad bowl, season well with salt and pepper.

Drain the anchovies and cut the fillets in half lengthways, quarter the eggs lengthways and add both to the salad with the olives. Spoon over the vinaigrette and toss the salad. Sprinkle with parsley and serve with French bread.

*Gratin dauphinois**

Gratin of Potatoes Baked in Milk

Serves 4

This can be used as either a main or a side dish. French potatoes tend to be waxy, which is why they are so difficult to purée. This delicious potato dish

Summer fare: salade niçoise

makes the most of their ability to maintain their shape.
Part-cooking the potatoes in a saucepan speeds up the cooking time of this dish, which can otherwise take as long as 2 hours. You can, if you prefer, simply arrange the potato pieces in an earthenware dish, dot them with the butter, pour in the milk and mix, then cook the gratin for 1¾–2 hours in a cool oven. Parmesan can be substituted for the Gruyère and it will give a much stronger flavour but the result is not, then, authentically French. Gruyère is often sold ready-grated in packets in French supermarkets. To make a main course for lunch, add more than the suggested 50g/2oz of cheese.

500g/1lb potatoes, peeled
250ml/9fl oz milk
50g/2oz unsalted butter
250ml/9fl oz cream, crème fraîche or thick Greek-style yoghurt
salt and freshly ground black pepper
grated nutmeg
1 clove garlic
25g/1oz butter, to grease
50g/2oz Gruyère cheese, grated

Slice the potatoes thinly into rounds, using the slicing attachment of a food processor or a *mandoline*, if you have one. Rinse them well to get rid of excess starch as this will make them stick together. Bring the milk to the boil in a large pan. Stir in the unsalted butter, potatoes and cream, then season with salt, pepper and grated nutmeg to taste. Stir carefully with a wooden spoon, separating the potato slices as you go. Bring slowly to the boil and cook over a low heat for 30 minutes.
Set the oven at 160°C, 325°F, gas 3. Meanwhile, rub the sides of an earthenware dish with the garlic, then butter the sides of the dish. Pour in the potato mix and sprinkle the top with the grated Gruyère. Cook in the oven for about 45 minutes. If liked, put under a grill for a minute or two to brown the top to a deep golden colour.

*Pipérade**

Scrambled Eggs with Peppers

Serves 4

A quick, easy and cheap lunch dish from the Basque country which is a scrambled version of a Spanish omelette. You can add other ingredients – chopped ham for instance or pieces of bacon, or chopped cooked potato – to make the dish even more filling. Incorporate these extra ingredients at the same time as the onion and, if necessary, add a little more oil. If you prefer, substitute a green pepper in place of one of the red ones.

2 red peppers, seeded
8 eggs
salt and freshly ground black pepper
2 tablespoons olive oil
1 large onion, skinned and chopped
2 cloves garlic, skinned and crushed
500g/1lb tomatoes, skinned and chopped

Slice the peppers into strips, then chop them into shorter lengths. Beat the eggs together in a bowl with a little salt and pepper.
Heat the oil in a large, heavy pan and cook the onion over a low heat until it is golden brown. Stir in the garlic, then push the mixture to one side. Tilt the pan so that the oil runs down, then add the peppers and cook them for a minute or two. Add the tomatoes and stir the vegetables together. Cook over a low heat for about 8 minutes or until they have all softened, some of the moisture has evaporated and the mixture has firmed up a little.

Ratatouille *is a versatile dish*

Pour in the eggs, and stir them in. Continue to cook the mixture, stirring gently (do not overdo it or it will go an unpleasant grey-brown colour). The moment the underneath is set and the top is thick and creamy, take the pan off the heat and allow the *pipérade* to finish cooking by its own heat. Serve with crusty French bread.

*Ratatouille***

Provençal Vegetable Ragoût

Serves 6

A great Provençal dish that is, basically, a mix of vegetables stewed in olive oil. It can be eaten hot or cold, as a side dish or a main course – with fried eggs on top, for instance, for lunch. Ratatouille actually improves after a night spent in the refrigerator. Purists sometimes cook each vegetable separately, then stir them together at the last minute. This way is quicker. The essential ingredients are tomatoes, aubergines, onions, peppers, courgettes, garlic and olive oil. But you can vary the recipe by adding mushrooms or even olives.

2 aubergines
2 courgettes
3 large tomatoes
6 tablespoons olive oil
3 large onions, skinned and chopped
2 large peppers, seeded and sliced
2 cloves garlic, skinned and crushed

Prepare the aubergines and courgettes ahead of time. First, slice them into thin rounds. Sprinkle with salt, then put them in a colander with a weighted plate on top. Leave to drain over a bowl or in the sink.
Skin the tomatoes by nicking their skins, then plunging them into boiling water and leaving them there for a moment. Remove the skins, then chop the tomatoes.
Heat the oil in a large heavy pan with a lid and fry the onion until it has coloured. Add the peppers and garlic, then the drained aubergines and courgettes. Finally, add the chopped tomatoes. When the mixture is bubbling, put the lid back on the pan, turn down the heat and simmer until soft – about 45 minutes. Serve hot one day with crusty bread, cold the next.

*Coquilles Saint-Jacques au gratin***

Scallop Gratin

Serves 4

Coquilles Saint-Jacques (scallops) can be cooked very simply in their shells just by dotting them with butter and breadcrumbs and cooking them in the oven for about 20 minutes. This recipe is a little more elaborate and makes a more filling dish. If you are making it at home, from frozen scallops, you can serve the scallops in large ramekins if you do not have any shells. The cheese and breadcrumb topping can be omitted if you do not have a grill.

8 scallops in their shells
450ml/¾ pint milk
25g/1oz butter
4 tablespoons plain flour
75g/3oz hard cheese, finely grated
salt and freshly ground black pepper
2 tablespoons double cream, thick yoghurt or crème fraîche (optional)

For the topping:
50g/2oz breadcrumbs
25g/1oz hard cheese, grated

Prise open the scallops and remove the black sac. Scrub and dry four deep shells. Trim the white part of the scallops then rinse and drain it along with the red coral. Cut into small pieces and season. Place in a saucepan with the milk and simmer for 5 minutes or until just firm. Drain, reserving the milk, and keep warm.
Melt the butter in another pan, add the flour, and cook for 2 minutes stirring carefully to avoid browning. Lower the heat and gradually stir in the reserved milk. Bring to the boil and cook until the sauce thickens, stirring all the time. Stir in the 75g/3oz cheese, then check the seasoning. If the sauce becomes lumpy blend it or beat with a wire whisk.
Pile the scallops back into four shells. Stir the cream, yoghurt or crème fraîche into the sauce and generously coat the scallops with it. Sprinkle with a mix of the breadcrumbs and cheese for the topping. Then brown under a hot grill.

*Cassoulet***

Haricot Bean Casserole with Pork and Lamb

Serves 6

This famous haricot bean stew is from Languedoc. The name comes from cassol, *the southwestern French dialect word for the clay cooking pot traditionally used for the dish. Eat cassoulet, and you realise why the French make lunch the main meal of the day, for it is far too heavy to digest in the evening. This is one of those dishes that improves on reheating. It is vital to use real white haricot beans to obtain the right flavour. Preserved goose* (CONFIT D'OIE) *is widely sold in food shops throughout France.*

500g/1lb white haricot beans
175g/6oz salt pork or a chunk of unsmoked bacon, such as knuckle
500g/1lb belly pork or pork spare rib, in large pieces
2 cloves garlic, skinned and crushed
bouquet garni
1 carrot, peeled
1 whole onion, skinned and stuck with 6 cloves
salt and freshly ground black pepper
50g/2oz goose fat or lard
350g/12oz preserved goose (*confit d'oie*)
1 onion, skinned and chopped
350g/12oz boned shoulder of lamb, cut into large chunks
250g/8oz garlic sausage or other similar sausage, cut into chunks
75g/3oz white breadcrumbs

Soak the haricot beans for an hour to soften them. Cut off any rind from the salt pork or bacon and belly or spare rib pork. Chop the rind into squares and set it aside for the time being.

Put the beans and salt pork or bacon in a large saucepan together with the garlic, bouquet garni, carrot and the onion stuck with cloves. Season, cover with water and simmer for 1½ hours.

Meanwhile, heat the goose fat in a frying pan and brown the preserved goose and chopped onion. Remove from the pan, then brown the pork and lamb pieces, adding a little extra fat if necessary. Reserve any remaining fat at the end of cooking.

Set the oven at 160°C, 325°F, gas 3. Remove the clove-studded onion from the saucepan and, using a slotted spoon, put the reserved bacon or pork rind in a large earthenware pot with a close-fitting lid. Cover with a layer of beans, meats, then more beans, then meat, topping the dish with chunks of garlic sausage.

Moisten the contents with some of the cooking broth. Cover and cook in the oven for 1½ hours, adding more broth occasionally if necessary to keep the mixture moist.

Finally, take the lid off the pan and sprinkle the top with the white breadcrumbs. Pour a little reserved goose fat from the frying pan over the top. Put the pot back in the oven for another 20 minutes, or until the top has formed a golden crust. Serve on its own.

Couscous, *a taste of the exotic*

*Couscous***

Serves 4–6

The sign 'Couscous aujourd'hui' *is found hanging in the windows of cafés and brasseries all over France. It signifies that the North African dish is being served, usually for lunch. The reason for its popularity is France's colonial history, linked as it is to Algeria and Morocco. Couscous is extremely filling and very tasty. If you want a lighter dish, or want to save cash, remove the chicken and lamb from the recipe, add green peppers and aubergines and you have* couscous aux sept légumes *instead. The couscous itself, which is actually rolled semolina, can be found in shops in an easy-cook (*toute prête*) version all over France in distinctive red, white and blue packets.* HARISSA, *the red chilli sauce, can also be bought ready made in cans or tubes.*

50g/2oz dried chick-peas (*pois chiches*) or 1 (400g/14oz) can
2 tablespoons olive oil
1kg/2lb neck of lamb
2 large onions, skinned and chopped
2 turnips, peeled and quartered
2 carrots, peeled and sliced
a few saffron strands or 2 teaspoons ground turmeric
salt and freshly ground black pepper
4 chicken joints (breast or leg), skinned
2 courgettes, chopped
125g/4oz broad beans (canned if necessary)
2 tomatoes, skinned and chopped

For the couscous:
75g/3oz raisins
500g/1lb easy-cook couscous
25g/1oz butter or 1 tablespoon oil
50g/2oz flaked almonds

For the harissa:
1 teaspoon chilli powder
1 small can tomato purée

Put the chick-peas to soak the night before if you are using dried ones. Heat the oil in a large heavy saucepan and brown the lamb lightly. Add the chick-peas, onions, turnips and carrots and cover generously with water. Bring to the boil and add the pounded saffron or turmeric with seasoning. Simmer, skimming the top from time to time if necessary to remove scum. After 30 minutes, put the chicken joints into the broth, adding more water if necessary to cover them. Bring back to the boil; cook for a further 30 minutes.
Meanwhile, prepare the couscous: take a ladleful of broth and pour it over the raisins to plump them up. Measure out the couscous in cupfuls and put it in a bowl. Add exactly the same amount of boiling water by volume – if you use 4 cups of couscous, add 4 cups of water. Stir in the butter or oil with a fork and leave for 15 minutes for the grains to swell. Then stir in the drained plumped raisins and almonds. Add the courgettes, broad beans and tomatoes to the stew and bring back to the boil. Fluff the grains of couscous with a fork. Ladle them into a sieve or fine colander (line one with scalded muslin if necessary) and sit it in the top of the saucepan, wrapping a folded tea towel under the rim if necessary to stop it dipping into the liquid. Cook for a further 30 minutes. (If you have difficulty in locating a sieve, the couscous can be served a different way – simply heated gently in a saucepan, but it will not be so fluffy.) Finally, to make the harissa, take a ladleful of stew and stir in the chilli powder and a little tomato purée to thicken and colour it. Put this into a small bowl.
To serve, offer around the couscous (which is eaten like rice) and the stew separately, then pass the harissa. The latter is extremely peppery and should be added by each person, drop by drop to their stew until it is fiery enough for them.

*Poulet à l'estragon**

Chicken with Tarragon

Serves 4

This simple dish, which comes from Lyonnais, is basically roast chicken – but vive la différence! *If you think the children might not like the slightly aniseed-like tarragon flavour, leave the herb butter off part of the chicken, the legs for instance, and serve them plain instead. If the chicken comes without giblets, use a chicken stock cube to flavour the sauce. And if you want a richer version, stir in a tablespoonful of thick cream into the gravy before serving.*

50g/2oz butter
3 tablespoons chopped fresh tarragon or 1½ tablespoons dried
1.5kg/3lb chicken with giblets
salt and freshly ground black pepper
2 tablespoons butter or oil, for cooking

Set the oven at 180°C, 350°F, gas 4. Soften the 50g/2oz butter and pound it with the tarragon using a pestle and mortar or with the back of a metal spoon. Remove the giblets from the chicken. Working your fingers gently under the skin of the chicken breast and lifting it as you go, spread a layer of the tarragon mix over the flesh. If there is any over, put the rest inside the chicken. Cover the breast of the bird with foil. Melt the 2 tablespoons butter or oil in a baking tin and put in the bird. Roast for 1 hour, removing the foil towards the end so that the breast turns golden brown. Meanwhile, to make stock, place the giblets from the bird with 300ml/½ pint water in a saucepan. Simmer until the liquid is reduced by half. When the chicken is done, remove it from the pan, tipping the bird so that the tarragon flavoured juices run into the pan. Pour in the strained giblet stock and bring to the boil. Strain again and serve with the bird.

Note: To check that the chicken is cooked, pierce the meat at the thickest part (behind the thighs) with the point of a knife. If the juices run clear and there are no signs of pink flesh, the bird is cooked; if there is any blood or pink meat visible, then cook the chicken a little longer. It is a good idea to check the bird about three-quarters of the way through cooking, particularly if you are using an oven which is unfamiliar, as overcooked chicken is disappointing.

Poulet à l'estragon, *roast chicken with a flavour of France*

Côte de porc normande*

Pork with Cider and Calvados

Serves 4

A quick pork dish from Normandy, using the produce of the countryside – Calvados and cider. You can also stir in cream at the last minute to make an even more delicious dish. In this recipe the chops are fried, but they could equally well be grilled or baked in the oven, provided you are able to catch the juices to use them for the sauce. If grilling or baking, the apples can be cooked with the chops. Use shallots rather than onions if you can, as they give a more delicate flavour.

1 large clove garlic, skinned and halved
4 pork chops
4 shallots or 1 large onion, skinned and finely chopped
75g/3oz butter
salt and freshly ground black pepper
2 large cooking apples
300ml/½ pint cider
2 tablespoons calvados

Smear the cut clove of garlic over both sides of the pork chops. Cook the shallots or onion in 50g/2oz of the butter in a frying pan until softened. Add the chops and brown them on each side. Season, then lower the heat, cover and cook until the chops are tender – 20 minutes or more, according to their size.
Meanwhile core, but do not peel, the cooking apples, then cut them into thick rings. Poach them in the remaining butter in a separate pan.
Once the pork is cooked, lift out the chops and keep them warm while you prepare the sauce. Pour the cider into the frying pan and bring it to the boil, stirring in the juices from the meat and the shallots. Let it bubble fast to reduce it a little and thicken it slightly. Add the calvados and bring back to the boil. Pour the sauce over the chops and serve, together with the apple rings.

*Lapin à la dijonnaise**

Rabbit in Mustard Sauce

Serves 4

Rabbits are widely available in France, they are usually cheap and they have a pleasant gamey flavour. Roast rabbit, like roast turkey, tends to be rather dry, so anoint it with butter first, then top it with foil. You must use real Dijon mustard, which is readily available abroad as well as in France. The more fiery English version would make this recipe unpalatable. Traditionally, the rabbit is cooked whole, but you could joint it, reducing the baking time to 40 minutes. If you do not like rabbit, try substituting chicken instead, or pork chops, but leave out the marinade.

1 oven-ready rabbit
250ml/8fl oz vinegar
50g/2oz butter
1 small pot Dijon mustard
2 tablespoons oil
175ml/6fl oz crème fraîche, Greek-style yoghurt or double cream

Put the rabbit in a small oven dish, pour over the vinegar and leave overnight to marinate, turning it from time to time, initially. This helps to make the flesh tastier and more tender. Set the oven at 190°C, 375°F, gas 5. Drain the rabbit, pat dry and smear it with the butter. Coat it liberally with mustard and place whole in a baking dish with the oil. Cover the rabbit with a piece of foil to stop it becoming too dry. Roast for about an hour (according to size); to test whether it is cooked, spike with a sharp knife to check that the juices are no longer pink. Remove the rabbit when it is cooked, put it on one side and keep warm. Drain off some of the fat if there seems to be too much, then stir the remainder, scraping up the juices from the bottom of the pan. Spoon in the crème fraîche over a very low heat. Do not boil or it may curdle. Check the sauce for flavour, add more mustard if necessary. Pour over the rabbit and serve.

*Clafoutis**

Baked Cherry Pudding

Serves 6

This is a classic French dessert which comes from Limousin. It is a splendid show-off item at a dinner party. You can used canned cherries for the dish if fresh ones are not in season, or substitute apples instead. This batter tart looks, and behaves, just like a Yorkshire pudding in that it puffs up, then sinks. It can be served hot, cold or just lukewarm, cut in wedges. A sweet dessert wine like Beaumes de Venise or Sauternes goes well with it.

25g/1oz butter, for greasing
125g/4oz plain flour
pinch of salt
100g/3½oz castor sugar
2 eggs
170ml/6fl oz milk
1 tablespoon dark rum (optional)
500g/1lb black cherries, stoned

Set the oven at 180°C, 350°F, gas 4. Butter a 20cm/8in shallow baking tin (best) or flan dish (a loose-bottomed flan tin will leak) and put it in the oven to heat. Put the flour, salt and half the sugar into a bowl. Beat the eggs, one at a time, and add to the mixture. Then slowly add the milk, beating it to a smooth batter. Alternatively, you can use a blender for this process. Stir in the rum. Leave the mixture on one side to rest while you stone the cherries. Take the tin from the oven, pour in the mixture and spoon in the

Clafoutis, *cherry batter pudding*

fruit. Bake for 45 minutes – 1 hour. To test if the *clafoutis* is ready, pierce it with the point of a metal skewer; the skewer should come out clean. Remove from the oven, turn out the *clafoutis* and dust it with the rest of the sugar.

*Tarte au citron***

Lemon Flan

Serves 6–8

French rich shortcrust pastry (pâte sablée) *is sweeter and more substantial than ordinary shortcrust but you could, of course, substitute the latter. The filling tastes pleasantly sharp.*

For the pastry:
200g/7oz plain flour
pinch of salt
1 tablespoon castor sugar
125g/4oz butter
1 egg

For the filling:
5 eggs
125g/4oz castor sugar
75g/3oz butter, melted
finely grated rind of 2 lemons and juice of 4 lemons.

Set the oven at 180°C, 350°F, gas 4. For the pastry, sift the flour into a bowl with the salt and sugar. Cut the butter into small pieces and mix it in with a fork until the mixture looks like fine breadcrumbs. Beat the egg with about 2 tablespoons cold water and work into the mixture, adding a little more water if necessary. Work the pastry into a ball, then roll out and use to line a 25cm/10in flan tin.
For the filling, whisk the eggs and sugar together in a bowl until fluffy. Add the melted butter, lemon rind and lemon juice. Pour the mixture into the flan case. Bake for 35–40 minutes until the pastry is golden and the filling set.

Tarte au citron, *lemon flan*

SPECIAL EVENTS AND SEASONAL FOODS

France has a fair number of public holidays. In fact, there are certain times of the year when the country comes to a virtual standstill – apart from the ubiquitous *boulangeries* (bakers) and the restaurants, which will be packed out with French families. Those holidays to note are Easter Monday, Ascension Day and Whit Monday, all moveable dates according to the year's calendar, then May Day (1 May), and Victory Day (8 May). Bastille Day is celebrated on the 14 July, and Assumption Day, on 15 August, is another public holiday. All Saints' Day, 1 November, is a big, if rather sombre, event, when it is a custom to put chrysanthemums on the family graves. On that day and the days around it, the cemeteries are full of colour and rows of potted flowers stand outside florists' shops. Armistice Day is commemorated on 11 November with all the fervour of a country which suffered the horrors of enemy occupation. In addition to these national dates, there are likely to be local celebrations of some sort or another from time to time. The best way to find out about these is to enquire at the *Syndicat d'Initiative*, the tourist office, in the nearest town. Most of them issue a calendar of events in their area. They are also very helpful in other ways – recommending places to visit, giving bus times and so on. There are also esoteric food festivals worth seeing – the pink garlic festival at Lautrec, in Tarn in August, for instance. There are fig auctions at Saint-Vaast-la-Hogue, Normandy in October, and a strawberry feast in Plougastel, Brittany, on the third Sunday in June. There is also a grape festival in Sancerre, Loire in August. Wine festivals abound and, apart from the great auctions at Beaune in November, Sancerre has a wine fair in June, and there is a national one in August. Lisle-sur-Tarn has one in July, and *Wine Festivals Gaillac* hold another there in August. There are also a whole host of such festivals during August in the Languedoc–Roussillon area. In fact you can be sure that all wine-growing areas celebrate in some way or other during the summer or autumn. On a more humble scale – but just as much fun – is the beer festival at Domfront, Orne, in July. Agricultural shows, like the big events in Tours in September and Auch, Gascony in October, are well worth taking a look at. So is the fair at Lessay, Normandy, in September, which is renowned for its huge barbecues, when whole animals are spit-roasted. Gastronomic festivals can be found too, like the one at Sauveterre-de- Guyenne, Aquitaine, in July.

Foods in Season

Normandy

Early summer: cherries from Honfleur region.
Summer: strawberries (May, June, August, September), raspberries from Caen area (June, July, September–October),

redcurrants, blackcurrants (June–August).
Autumn: figs (October), pears (September–October).

Brittany
Spring and early summer: artichokes (January–May), strawberries (May, June, August, September).
Autumn: cauliflowers (September–May).

Champagne and Ile-de-France
Winter and spring: endive, leeks.
Early summer: petits pois.
Autumn: celeriac, pumpkins.

Alsace and Lorraine
Spring and early summer: asparagus (April–May), cherries (May–July), strawberries (May, June, August, September).
Summer: plums (July–September), raspberries (June, July, September, October).
Autumn: apples, quinces, wild mushrooms, wild strawberries.

The Loire
Spring and summer: artichokes (January–May), asparagus (April–July), courgettes, cucumbers, beefsteak tomatoes, blackcurrants (June–August), hazelnuts (fresh, July–September), raspberries (June, July, September, October), strawberries (May, June, August, September), celery (July–October).
Autumn: fennel, saffron, walnuts, apples (Granny Smith, from October–April), pears (Conference, from October–April), mushrooms.

Burgundy and Franche-Comté
Early summer: asparagus from Auxonne.
Summer: blackcurrants (June–August), cherries, raspberries, Jerusalem artichokes.

Bordeaux and the Dordogne
Spring: artichokes (January–May), courgettes, cucumbers, large Marmande tomatoes, new potatoes, kiwi fruit (December–May).
Summer: asparagus, aubergines (May–November), haricots verts, peppers, strawberries (May, June, August, September), greengages, melons, peaches (June–September), nectarines, plums (July–September), peppers (June–September).
Autumn: chestnuts (October, November), hazelnuts (fresh, July–September), pears (Conference, from October–April), walnuts (from October–January), grapes, mushrooms.

Auvergne and Limousin
Early summer: strawberries.
Summer: hazelnuts, plums, raspberries (June–July, September–October), lentils from Le Puy, apricots (June–August), Jerusalem artichokes, greengages, mulberries, plums (July–September).
Autumn: chestnuts (October–November), walnuts, apples, mushrooms.

Rhône and Dauphine Savoie
Spring and early summer: garlic, wild mushrooms.
Summer: apricots (June–August), cherries (May–July), apples, black and redcurrants (June–August), greengages, melons, nectarines (May–September), raspberries (June, July, September, October), peaches (June–September), cardoons, almonds (June and July).
Autumn: chestnuts, walnuts (October–February), pears

(Williams, June–September, Conference, October–April), grapes (August–November), apples (Golden Delicious, Red Delicious, October–April).

Gascony, Tarn and Languedoc
Spring and early summer: artichokes (January–May), asparagus, aubergines, cherries, nectarines (May–September), peaches (June–September), strawberries (May, June, August, September), courgettes.
Summer: peppers, garlic, almonds, apples, apricots (June–August), greengages, melons, pears, plums (July–September), wild mushrooms, hazelnuts (fresh, July–September).
Autumn: celery, leeks, chestnuts (October–November), grapes, strawberries, walnuts, pumpkins.

Provence
Spring and early summer: artichokes (January–May), courgettes (April–October), aubergines (May–November), peppers (July–September), tomatoes, cherries (from the Vaucluse, May–July), melons (May–October), strawberries (May, June, August, September), asparagus (April–July), aubergines (May–November).
Summer: garlic, shallots, apricots (June–August), nectarines (May–September), peaches (July–September), pears (Williams, June–September), plums (July–September), wild mushrooms, figs, Swiss chard, peppers (June–September).
Late summer and autumn: grapes (August–November), cardoons, fennel (November–February).

Fresh almonds of early summer

EATING OUT

One of the great pleasures of holidaying in France is to linger over a meal in a restaurant after a busy day. The vast number and variety of places where you can eat can make the process of choosing bewildering. However, some of the most memorable meals are likely to be taken in a quiet country backwater, rather than in a busy city where parking may be difficult and prices high. The French have their main meal in the middle of the day. Shops, factories and schools close, then everyone heads for home, if they can, or to the local restaurant to linger over a meal.

Hours are more flexible in the larger cities, and there is far more choice of places to eat, whereas in a small town or village it may be difficult to get a snack between meals.
If you are travelling south to your destination, staying overnight in a small hotel, your mind may be made up for you, for some hotels insist that you dine there if you are staying for the night. You can always move on somewhere in protest, it is true, but by then you are usually too tired to argue. Some hotels, on the other hand, do not have restaurants. However, if you are roaming around town, wondering where to eat, be wary of an establishment that has no customers at all. In a place like France there must be a reason!

Restaurant

A *restaurant* in France, as in England, is a place for a full-blown meal. Most of them display a menu outside including a *menu touristique* (tourist menu) or special *plats du jour* (dishes of the day), both can be a good, economical choice.

Auberge

An *auberge* is basically supposed to be a country restaurant, usually combined with a hotel, serving full meals.

Hostellerie

A *hostellerie* is very similar to an *auberge* often housed in an ancient building. However, in large cities these words are often used to help give a fake country air to what may be a modern town restaurant.

Rôtisserie

A *rôtisserie* is a restaurant that technically specialises in spit-roasted or charcoal-grilled food.

Bistro

Going down the social scale, a *bistro* or *bistrot*, is a cross between a restaurant and café, the sort of place where you could get away with just eating one course. Service is usually quick and the food cheap but you may be jammed in, knee to knee, for these eateries are usually in premises too small to call themselves restaurants.

Relais Routier

For a good meal at a cheap price but possibly no choice of main dish try a *relais routier*. You might not think of stopping at a pull-up for lorry drivers at home, but in France there is quite a difference.

Opening Times

A tip for discovering restaurant opening hours is to keep an eye on the local shops; as they close for lunch the restaurants will open. In the south, meals tend to be served a little later in the evening than elsewhere. If you have a small child with you, you may find it difficult to get anything to eat in the evening before 19.00 hrs.

Café

Cafés serve both alcoholic and soft, hot and cold drinks, including delights like *citron pressé* (fresh lemon juice with water and sugar). You should also be able to get croissants and simple snacks at most of them. It is part of the French way of life to spend anything up to an hour over one drink in a

Relax over a drink in the café

café, so the waiter will not hassle you. Equally, if you want to get away quickly, pay for your drink when he brings it to you, or you may have difficulty in catching his eye for the bill.

Salon de thé
A *salon de thé* is usually a quite elegant place in a shopping area, sometimes attached to a *pâtisserie*, where you can order rather weak tea and try some delicious cakes. The tea will be served with lemon, incidentally, unless you specifically ask for milk. Tea is *thé*, *thé au citron* is lemon tea, *thé à la menthe* – if you want to try it – is peppermint tea, reckoned to be good for the digestion.

Brasserie or Buffet
If you are taking a meal out of normal hours, while travelling by car for instance, you can always get something to eat at a *brasserie* in a large town or in a *buffet* at a station. It might be the last thing you would think of doing at home, but in France some first class meals can be had at a station buffet and many are Michelin rated.

Drug-stores
In the larger towns, *drug-stores* serve meals at all times. The words *casse-croûte* mean snack, and if the words *à toutes heures* are alongside, you know you are in luck, because food is served at all hours.

Quick and Cheap
If you are in a hurry, merely using food as fuel, or having to count the francs carefully, then head for the *libre-service* (self-service) cafeterias in a supermarket, or on the autoroutes. Pizza places can be found all over France, especially in the south, and *crêperies* are a good choice for a quick cheap meal. McDonald's and other fast food

chains have opened up all over the country too. If you just want a drink and a sandwich, then look for a *buvette* where you will probably stand up to eat or take your purchase away with you. Never insult the proprietor of a full-blown restaurant by telling him you are in a hurry, he simply would not understand your attitude.

If you are on the move, and do not want to stop for long, then it is best to take a picnic lunch rather than queue up at a crowded *libre-service* or have a long wait in a restaurant.

Though the motorway cafés do not go in for great cuisine, the food is perfectly adequate and service is quick – usually you will find both a restaurant and a snack bar.

Signs of the value of good food

For Breakfast

You may be served with the traditional French breakfast at your hotel as part of the price of your room for the night. *Café complet*, as it is called, varies according to the standard of the hotel and the price of the room, from fresh orange juice, a basket of croissants and brioches plus a choice of *confiture*, to reheated *café* with milk and toasted pieces of yesterday's bread with no choice of jam. If you haven't paid for breakfast in advance, and it looks disappointing, then simply take yourselves off to the nearest café and breakfast there. The croissants are sure to be fresh and still warm, the coffee better.

Booking a Table

There is nothing more disappointing than to arrive at the restaurant of your choice, only to find it is *complet* (full). So if you are planning a special meal out, it is as well to phone and book in advance (your hotel will do it for you if necessary). Sunday lunchtime is a favourite with French families for taking a meal out, especially in the country, so it is important to book then; also on public holidays and other days that may catch you napping, like Bastille Day (14 July) for instance, when the whole town will go out *en fête* with brass bands, fireworks, the lot, and everyone eats out *en famille*.

Remember to be prompt if you reserve a table; if you are more than, say, 10 minutes late, your table is likely to have been given to someone else.

The Menu

Having chosen your restaurant, you will need to make your choice of food, either choosing the most expensive way, from *à la carte* dishes shown on the *carte* (menu), or from the *table d'hôte* (literally, the table of the host), a menu with a smaller choice. There may be a *prix fixe* menu too, with a choice of courses. Go for the *plat du jour* or the *spécialité de la maison* if you want to try something local. Most restaurants will also have a *menu touristique*, boring food at a reasonable price – probably pork chop or steak and *frites* (chips). Or for those who want a real blow-out, try the *menu gastronomique*, the most expensive one on the *carte*, with extra courses and more flamboyant food.

If you see no price but the letters SG (*selon grosseur*) against a dish – often something like lobster – then it is sold by size or weight, and it is as well to ask the price in advance. If the words *service compris* or *service et taxes compris* appears at the bottom of the menu, it is not necessary to leave a tip, though it is polite to leave a few coins at least from your change. Dishes usually arrive *garni*, with a small selection of vegetables on the plate. If you order a vegetable specifically, it may be served as a separate course.

Eating Out

two coffees, please deux cafés, s'il vous plaît *deu kafay seel voo pleh*

can I have a receipt? donnez-moi un reçu, s'il vous plaît, *donnay mwa uN Reussew seel voo pleh*

here's your receipt voici votre reçu *vwassi votReu Reussew*

what time do you serve meals? à quelle heure servez-vous les repas? *a kel euR seRvay voo leh Reupa?*

I prefer non-smoking je préfère 'pour non fumeurs' *zheu pRefehR pooR nawN fewmeuR*

is there a car park? y a-t-il un parking? *ee ateel uN paRkeeng?*

where are the toilets? où sont les WC? *oo sawN leh doobleuvayssay?*

may I (we) sit down? je peux m'asseoir? (on peut s'asseoir)? *zheu peuh masswaR? (awN peuh sasswaR?)*

the menu, please le menu, s'il vous plaît *leu meunew seel voo pleh*

dish of the day le plat du jour *leu pla dew zhooR*

soup soupe, potage *soop, potahzh*

first course premier plat *pReumyay pla*

starter entrée *ahNtray*

vegetables légumes *legewm*

seafood crustacés *kRewstassay*

grills plats grillés *pla gReeyay*

dessert dessert *dessaiR*

pastries pâtisserie *pateesRee*

ice-cream glace *glass*

fruit fruit *fRwee*

I would like to book a table for four j'aimerais réserver une table pour quatre *zhehmReh ReseRvay ewn tableu pooR katR*

how is it cooked? c'est préparé comment? *seh pRepaRay kommahN?*

baked cuit (au four) *kwi (oh fooR)*

boiled (poached) bouilli (poché) *booyee (poshay)*

fried frit *fRee*

grilled grillé *gReeyay*

roast rôti *Rotee*

sautéed sauté *sohtay*

steamed cuit à la vapeur *kwee ta la vapeuR*

what do you recommend? que recommandez-vous? *keu ReukommahNday voo?*
what is this, that? qu'est-ce que c'est? *keskeusseh?*
a small portion une petite portion *ewn peuteet poRsyawN*
may I change my order? je peux changer la commande? *zheu peuh shahNzhay la kommahNd?*
can we have some more bread? encore un peu de pain s'il vous plaît *ahNkoR uN peu deu paN seel voo pleh*

Paying the Bill

the bill, please l'addition s'il vous plaît *ladissyawN seel voo pleh*
is service included? le service est compris? *leu seRvees eh kawNpRee?*
what is the charge? combien je vous dois? *kawNbyaN zheu voo dwa?*
do you accept credit cards? vous acceptez les cartes de crédit? *voo zakseptay leh kaRt deu kRedee?*
thank you, this is for you merci, et ceci est pour vous/(c'est bon) *meRsee . . . ay seussee eh pooR voo/(seh bawN)*
we enjoyed it, thank you nous avons trouvé très bon, merci *noo zavawN tRoovay tReh bawN, meRsee*
nothing else, thank you rien d'autre, merci *RyaN dohtR meRsee*

Drinks

On the drinks front, unless you want something special, the *vin de pays* or *vin de table* is a perfectly adequate, inexpensive choice of wine. If you order *eau minérale* they will want to know whether you want it *gazeuse* (sparkling) or *non-gazeuse,* otherwise do not be ashamed to ask simply for *de l'eau.* Drinking water in France is, on the whole, pure.

Ordering Drinks

a bottle of mineral water une bouteille d'eau minérale *ewn bootehy doh meeneRal*
a glass of white wine un verre de blanc *uN vaiR deu blahN*
a bottle of red wine une bouteille de rouge *ewn bootehy deu Roozh*
a half bottle une demi-bouteille *ewn deumee bootehy*
sparkling wine du vin mousseux *dew vaN moosseuh*
fruit juice un jus de fruit *uN zhew deu fRwee*
iced water de l'eau glacé *deuloh glassay*
fizzy lemonade de la limonade *deu la leemonad*
tea with lemon, milk du thé avec du citron/du lait *dew teh avek dew seetRawN/dew leh*
would you like some coffee? vous prenez du café? *voo pReunay dew kafay?*

CHILDREN

With the advent of disposable nappies and canned and packet baby food, travelling with a child in France is no more difficult than anywhere else. Most of the favourite brands of food, nappies and toiletries can be found in the supermarkets. And, for older children, things like cornflakes and ketchup are also available without any problem.
However, it seems a shame to take children abroad without giving them a chance to enjoy local regional food. Children can have amazingly sophisticated tastes – I have known toddlers who loved *moules à la marinière* and *escargots* (snails), for instance. It is often the older child who is

Eating out en famille *is the norm*

more finicky. So it is a good idea to prepare the children in advance by adding one or two French dishes to their ordinary menu at home, to acclimatise them to the taste, say, of garlic. It is a good idea, too, to take them out for a meal or two back home, if they are not used to restaurants.

Children are generally accepted anywhere in France, though if you are going to a really high-class restaurant it is as well to check first that a child will be welcome. It probably will be fine, though a certain standard of behaviour will be expected – playing hide and seek among the tables, for instance, would definitely not be appreciated.

If you are travelling with a small, very active, child, you probably will not want to eat in the hushed silence of a grand restaurant – though the proprietor will probably come rushing up with a series of *coussins* (cushions) or a high chair. French children seem to have an inbuilt attitude towards meals that makes them able to sit gravely through a four course dinner with *grandpère* and *grandmère*, while ours would grizzle, whine and want to get down. So if you are dealing with a fractious, travel-tired toddler and worried about behaviour problems, make it easy for yourself and either choose a self-service or fast-food place, or better still, a restaurant with tables in the garden, where they can run round as much as they like, while you enjoy a meal. Certainly a place that has paper table-cloths rather than the damask variety is less nerve-racking.

If necessary order a plate of chips (*frites*) immediately, or a strategic ice-cream (*glace*) for the child while you are still on your main course. The French will quite understand. A colouring book or a bag full of small toys are also useful distractions for small children who are going to have to sit patiently through a long meal. Another bag with a damp flannel in it for clean-ups of face and fingers afterwards is also useful. It is a good idea, anyway, if you have children on board, to take a constant supply of snacks in case the restaurant hunt goes on longer than you had expected.

Despite the fact that French water is perfectly *potable* (drinkable), a possible tummy upset for a toddler is not worth the risk. So pick a brand of mineral water that the child will drink, and have some to hand at all times. It is best to take an emergency kit of any medicines the children might need, for example, something for earache, upset tummy, sore throat and any other minor ailments. Your doctor can prescribe or suggest something suitable. Should a mild tummy upset occur, switch to mainly carbohydrate items like rice, together with natural yoghurt, for a few days; keep away from foods like meat which are more difficult to digest.

If you are travelling by plane, take some boiled sweets for small children to suck during take-off and landing to help prevent earache that sometimes comes on due to the change in pressure. Some airlines supply them, others do not.

Take a favourite toy or two to help settle a toddler down. And if you are travelling out of the hot season, a hot water bottle might not go amiss, for nights can be very cold and not many holiday houses have central heating; also smaller hotels are inclined to be mean over switching it on.

If you are self-catering, once installed in your villa or *gîte*, let the older children do some simple shopping, going to the *boulangerie* to get the breakfast bread, for instance. Encourage them to learn a few words of French, even if it is only *bonjour* and *au revoir*. They also enjoy visits to the market, and comparing French names for familiar items in supermarkets. Enlist their help, so they enter into the spirit of the French holiday. You will find, too that very small children overcome the language barrier of their own accord and love to play with French children of their own age. Above all, remember that the French, like all Latin races, love children, so relax!

Babies and Children

please could you warm up the baby's bottle? s'il vous plaît, pouvez-vous chauffer le biberon? *seel voo pleh poovay voo shohffay leu beebRawN?*

may I have a glass of water, fruit juice? j'aimerais un verre d'eau, de jus de fruit *zhemReh uN vaiR doh, deu jewd fRwee*

have you got a high-chair, please? auriez-vous une chaise haute pour enfants? *oRyay voo ewn shehz oht pooR ahNFahN?*

a half portion of . . ., please une demi-portion de . . . s'il vous plaît *ewn deumee poRsyawN deu . . . seel voo pleh*

may I have a plate/spoon/fork j'aimerais une assiette/une cuillère/une fourchette *zhemReh* *ewn assyett, ewn kweeyaiR/ewn fooRshett*

can you bring some serviettes, please? apportez-nous des serviettes, s'il vous plaît
appoRtaynoo deh seRvyett, seel voo pleh

SPECIAL DIETS

If you are on a special diet of any kind, gluten free for instance, then you ought to try to pack basic food to take with you to France. Otherwise you are going to spend a long time tracking down what you want. If you are worried about cholesterol counts or simply trying to lose weight, low-fat products are now widely available in supermarkets. Even the famous *crème fraîche* can be bought in a low-fat version which tastes just the same as the ordinary kind and there are low-fat yoghurts around, too.
You can also buy frozen ready-to-heat diet meals in the shops.
Anyone who enjoys herbal tea will find that France has almost as varied a selection of *tisanes*, as they are called, as of wine. You will find them sometimes in *pharmacies*, otherwise in health food shops. Also look out for them at the local market, the traditional place for selling the ingredients for drinks of this kind. On a stall there will be little sacks of lime flowers (*tilleul*), of lemon verbena (*verveine*), and dried fruits too, like blackcurrants (*cassis*), and camomile, of course. Cherry stalks (*queues de cerises*) are a useful natural diuretic, while mint (*menthe*) is good for the digestion.

Camomile for a tisane or two

If you are likely to need any special medication, then get your doctor to write out the name in Latin, the universal language for pharmacists and physicians.
France is only just discovering health foods. But most towns of any reasonable size have health food shops where vegans, vegetarians, or anyone with special dietary wishes, should be able to buy most items they require. These shops are called variously *centre diététique, boutique de produits diététiques* or simply *aliments naturels*.
A point to watch if you are on a low-salt diet – some of the classic French mineral waters have a high salt content. The amount can easily be discovered

by reading the bottle labels carefully. The popular Evian and the lesser-known Charrier, if you can find it, are both sodium free. Evian has a slight diuretic effect so does Contrexéville (see page 81).

Special diets

I'm a vegetarian je suis végétarien *zheu swee vezhetaRyaN*
is there any meat in it? ce plat contient de la viande? *seu pla kawNtyaN deu la vyahNd?*
I am a diabetic je suis diabète *zheu zwee dyabeht*
I am allergic to shellfish les crustacés ne me conviennent pas *leh kRewstassay neu meu kawNvyenn pa*

A snack is not necessarily cheap

I cannot eat flour (milk, sugar) je ne digère pas la farine, (le lait, le sucre) *zheu neu deezhaiR pa la faReen (leu leh, leu sewkR)*
I am on a diet je suis un régime *zheu swee zuN Rezheem*

TIGHT BUDGET

Shopping in a supermarket for ordinary items means that you can keep things under control, totting up how much you are spending before you reach the check-out. Supermarket prices are, of course, cheaper too, and you will find that most of them now take credit cards.
Markets in France offer the best bargains – though the price difference is not so marked as in some places, because the French always go for quality rather than price. Do not be afraid to pick out just one aubergine, courgette, or whatever, if that is what you need. That way you avoid wastage – and the stall-holder will not mind.
Equally, it is quite possible to ask for just a *demi* (half a baguette) from a country *boulangerie* if that is all you need. Although the price of bread is likely to be the least of your worries, stale loaves can be revived if you sprinkle them with water and pop them in the oven. And toasted slices of yesterday's bread are perfectly acceptable for breakfast.
Ready-made dishes like quiches, and cooked dishes from the *traiteur* (take-away food shop), may look enticing but they are often amazingly pricey. Meat, in general, is a very expensive item in France.

The French, rightly, insist on the very best possible quality. So use it sparingly, in dishes with plenty of vegetables added.

Vegetables in season are very cheap, and can be exciting if you make them up into dishes such as RATATOUILLE (see recipe pages 102-3); so a switch to a mainly vegetarian menu will save cash. Protein can be supplied by adding pulses such as some of the infinite variety of dried haricot beans, or chick-peas (*pois chiches*), both of which need soaking overnight if bought dried.

The enticing look of the vegetables on sale may well inspire you to make some inexpensive filling soups which are wonderful at midday, especially if the weather is chilly. Sweat a chopped onion in some oil or butter, then add the vegetable of your choice, stock cubes and some water, then simmer until the vegetables are tender and – hey presto you have a soup. In summer, tomatoes are very cheap, and they may be used to make an excellent salad – good for lunch with plenty of bread (see recipe page 96) – or a wonderful fresh soup.

Eggs are also economical and can often be bought direct from farms. A hearty omelette, peasant style, with chopped cooked potato and onion in it, or a PIPÉRADE (see recipe page 101), will be nourishing and filling. If you keep away from the more esoteric cheeses, this is another cheap way to eat. Fruit is an inexpensive item, too, and is often sold by the tray at very low prices – if you are a large group, or two families together, this works out as an economical way to buy.

On the drinks front, a *Cave Co-operative* will give you the best wine for your money. Check out the price of beer, on the other hand, before you buy, as it can be relatively expensive since much of it is imported.

PRACTICAL TIPS

Self Catering

If you are renting a *gîte* or a villa, it pays to take a small survival kit with you. For even though all officially registered *gîtes* will be well-stocked, many villa owners assume that you are going to eat out, and although there may be generous amounts of crockery, the gadgets may be on the mean side. You are unlikely to find a kettle in your kitchen or tea cups and saucers either. Bring your own tea, too. In many places, the cooker works off butane gas bottles, so it is as well to note where the nearest supplier is – usually the local garage.

Transporting Food

Two key points always to remember when buying food abroad: firstly do not flout the regulations and restrictions on the type and quantity of goods to bring home. Secondly, avoid at all costs breaking common sense hygiene practices simply to transport a delicacy which may well be off after a long, warm car journey. Only transport perishable foods if you are confident that you can keep them fresh until you intend eating them. A bad stomach will kill a gourmet taste for a foreign delicacy.

LANGUAGE

General phrases

yes/no oui/non *wee/nawN*
please s'il vous plaît *seel voo pleh*
thank you (very much) merci (beaucoup) *meRsee (bokoo)*
hello/goodbye bonjour/au revoir *bawNzhooR/oRvwaR*
how are you? comment ça va? *kommahN sa va?*
delighted to meet you enchanté *ahNshahNtay*
this is my wife (husband) voici ma femme (mon mari) *vwassee ma famm (mawN maRee)*
good morning bonjour *bawNzhooR*
good evening (and good night) bonsoir *bawNswaR*
good night bonne nuit *bon nwee*
tomorrow demain *deumaN*
see you later à tout à l'heure *a too ta leuR*
what? quoi? *kwa?*
when? quand? *kahN?*
why? pourquoi? *pooRkwa?*
which? lequel?/laquelle? *leukell/lakell*
excuse me pardon! *paRdawN!*
I'm sorry excusez-moi *exkewzay mwa*
I don't know je ne sais pas *zheun seh pa*
can you repeat that, please? voulez-vous bien répéter cela, s'il vous plaît *voolay voo byaN Repetay seula, seel voo pleh*
is it far (near)? c'est loin (tout près)? *seh lwaN (too pReh)?*
can you help me? pouvez-vous m'aider? *poovay voo meday?*
I understand je comprends *zheu kawNprahN*
I don't understand je ne comprends pas *zheun kawNprahN*
I want to change these traveller's cheques je voudrais changer ces travellers *zheu voodReh shahNzhay seh tRavellaiR*
can I pay with this credit card? je peux payer avec cette carte? *zheu peuh pehyay avek set kaRt?*
what time does the bank open? la banque s'ouvre à quelle heure? *la bahNk soovR a kell euR?*
early/late tôt/tard *toh/taR*
sometimes quelquefois *kelkeufwa*
what is your name? comment vous appelez-vous? *kommahN voo zapplay voo?*
what is the time? quelle heure est-il? *kell euR eteel?*
please speak more slowly s'il vous plaît parlez plus lentement *seel voo pleh paRlay plew lahNteumahN*
please write it down je vous prie de l'écrire *zheu voo pRee deu lekReeR*
do you speak English? vous parlez anglais? *voo paRlay ahNgleh?*

Numerals

1 un *uN*
2 deux *deuh*
3 trois *tRwa*
4 quatre *katR*
5 cinq *saNk*
6 six *seess*
7 sept *set*
8 huit *weet*
9 neuf *neuf*
10 dix *deess*
11 onze *awNz*
12 douze *dooz*
15 quinze *kaNz*
20 vingt *vaN*
25 vingt-cinq *vaNsaNk*
30 trente *tRahNt*
40 quarante *kaRahNt*
50 cinquante *saNkahNt*
60 soixante *swassahNt*
70 soixante-dix *swassahNt deess*
80 quatre-vingt *katReuvaN*
90 quatre-vingt-dix *katReuvaN deess*
100 cent *sahN*
200 deux cents *deuh sahN*
1000 mille *meell*

Weights and measures
1kg un kilo *uN keeloh*
2kg deux kilos *deuh keeloh*
100g cent grammes *sahN gRamm*
200g deux cents grammes *deuh sahN gRamm*
1 litre un litre *uN leetR*
¾ trois quarts de . . . *tRwa kaR deu . . .*
½ un demi- . . . *uN deumee*
¼ un quart de . . . *uN kaR deu . . .*
a portion of une portion de . . . *ewn poRsyawN deu . . .*
a cup une tasse . . . *ewn tass*
a slice of une tranche de . . . *ewn tRahNsh deu*
a piece of un morceau de . . . *uN moRsoh deu . . .*
twice that deux fois cela *deuh fwa seula*
a dozen une douzaine de . . . *ewn doozehn deu . . .*

Hints on Pronouncing French

Vowels
1 *ai, e, ei, é,* are mostly pronounced like 'e' in 'Terry'. At the end of words, *é, ez, er, et* are usually spoken like the 'ay' in 'say'.
2 In some words, *e* is pronounced like 'e' in 'the' (this is written as 'eu' in the pronunciation guides).
3 *a* is pronounced like 'a' in 'past', but rather shorter.
4 *i* is pronounced like 'ee' in 'sheep' but shorter.
5 *o* is pronounced like 'o' in 'hot' or 'ow' in 'low' (these appear as 'o' and 'oh' respectively in the pronunciation guides). *oi* is pronounced 'wa'.
6 *ou* is pronounced like 'oo' in 'boot'.
7 *u* has no English equivalent. To practise the sound say: ooooo with rounded lips, then try to say eeeee without unrounding the lips (this sound is written as 'ew' in the pronunciation guides).

Nasal vowels
These have no equivalent in English. They are pronounced by shutting the passage from the mouth to the nose while pronouncing the vowel. You do not pronounce the 'n' (to indicate this the 'n' appears as 'N' in the pronunciation guides).
8 Thus: *an, en* are pronounced 'ahN'; *on* as 'awN'; *ain, ein, in* as 'aN' (the 'a' as in 'cat'); *un* as 'uN', eg, *un bon vin blanc* – uN bawN vaN blahN.

Consonants
Mostly like their equivalent in English, except:
9 *ch* is pronounced 'sh'.
10 *j* and *g* before *e* and *i* are pronounced like 's' in 'usual' (this appears as 'zh' in the pronunciation guides).
11 *r* is strongly pronounced at the back of the throat. It appears as 'R' in the pronunciation guides.
12 *gn* is pronounced like 'ni' in 'onion'.
13 *ill* and *ille* are pronounced with a 'y' sound as in 'beyond'. Consonants at the end of a word are mostly not pronounced.

Note: In French, syllables are almost equally stressed, though the final syllable may have a slightly stronger stress.

CONVERSION TABLES

NOTES ON USING THE RECIPES

Weights and measures are written in metric and imperial. Follow only one set of measures as they are not interchangeable.

Abbreviations

Metric

g – gram or gramme
kg – kilogram
ml – millilitre

Imperial

oz – ounce
lb – pound
fl oz – fluid oz

Metric/Imperial Weight Conversions

50g/2oz	350g/12oz
75g/3oz	500g/1lb
100g/4oz	700g/1½lb
150g/5oz	1kg/2lb
175g/6oz	1.5kg/3lb
250g/8oz	2kg/4lb

Metric/Imperial Fluid Conversions

125ml/4fl oz
150ml/¼ pint (5fl oz)
175ml/6fl oz
200ml/7fl oz
300ml/½ pint (10fl oz)
500ml/18fl oz
600ml/1 pint (20fl oz)
750ml/1¼ pints
1 litre/1¾ pints
2 litres/3½ pints

Spoon Measures

Spoon measures refer to the standard measuring spoons and all quantities are level unless otherwise stated. **Do not** use table cutlery and serving spoons instead of measuring spoons as their capacity varies.

½ teaspoon – 2.5ml
1 teaspoon – 5ml
1 tablespoon – 15ml (3 teaspoons)

Oven Temperatures

The following settings are used in the recipes, providing centigrade, Fahrenheit and gas settings. However, cooking facilities in holiday accommodation may be limited or oven settings may be different or unreliable, therefore watch dishes carefully when baking in unfamiliar appliances.

110°C, 225°F, gas ¼
120°C, 250°F, gas ½
140°C, 275°F, gas 1
150°C, 300°F, gas 2
160°C, 325°F, gas 3
180°C, 350°F, gas 4
190°C, 375°F, gas 5
200°C, 400°F, gas 6
220°C, 425°F, gas 7
230°C, 450°F, gas 8
240°C, 475°F, gas 9

American Measures and Terms

Liquids: Imperial/American

8fl oz – 1 cup
16fl oz – 2 cups
20fl oz (1 pint) – 1 pint or 2½ cups
¼ pint – ⅔ cup
½ pint – ½ pint

Solids Whole pounds and fractions of a pound are used for some ingredients, such as butter, vegetables and meat. Cup measures are used for storecupboard foods, such as flour, sugar and rice. Butter is also measured by sticks.

Imperial/American

Butter – 8oz/1 cup (2 sticks)
Cheese, grated hard – 4oz/1 cup
Flour – 4oz/1 cup
Haricot beans, dried – 6oz/1 cup
Mushrooms, sliced – 8oz/2½ cups
Olives, whole – 4oz/1 cup
Parmesan cheese, grated – 1oz/3 tablespoons, 2oz/⅓ cup
Peas, shelled – 4oz/1 cup
Raisins – 6oz/1 cup
Rice (uncooked) – 8oz/1 cup

INDEX

Page numbers in italics refer to recipes

The Automobile Association wishes to thank the following photographers for their assistance in the preparation of this book.

Eric Meacher was commissioned for the front cover and pages 97, 98, 100, 102, 105, 107, 109, 110.

The remaining pictures were taken by Barrie Smith with the exception of pages 54, 87 (Dave Austin) and page 76 (Rick Strange).

All pictures are held in the Association's own library (©AA Photo Library).